I HATE
YOU—
don't leave me

I HATE YOU — don't leave me

JEROLD J. KREISMAN, M.D. & HAL STRAUS

⚕ THE BODY PRESS
a division of
PRICE STERN SLOAN
Los Angeles

©1989 Jerold Jay Kreisman, M.D. and Hal Straus
Published by Price Stern Sloan, Inc.
360 North La Cienega Boulevard, Los Angeles, CA 90048

ISBN: 0-89586-659-5

10 9 8 7 6 5 4 3 2

Library of Congress Cataloging-in-Publication Data
Kreisman, Jerold Jay.
    I hate you, don't leave me: understanding the borderline person-
ality / Jerold Jay Kreisman, Hal Straus.
        p.   cm.
    Bibliography: p.
    Includes index.
    ISBN 0-89586-659-5
    1. Borderline personality disorders.   I. Straus, Hal.   II. Title.
RC569.5.B6K74   1989
616.89—dc19   89-605
                                                             CIP

As all things,
for Doody

Acknowledgments

So many people contributed to this book that to mention them all by name would make us sound uncomfortably like entertainers whose acceptance speeches drone on and on through television awards ceremonies. There are, however, a few people who must be named.

The hospital administration of St. John's Mercy Medical Center, St. Louis, and its CEO, John T. Farrell, and the Department of Psychiatry and its chairman, Duane Q. Hagen, M.D., provided unflagging support for this book, and more importantly, great understanding when the project seemed overwhelming and threatened to deter me from other obligations.

The staff of the medical center's Comprehensive Treatment Unit—the nurses, social workers, pastoral care workers, psychiatric counselors, and activities therapists—provided the supportive working milieu from which many of the ideas of this book emerged. Without this staff of dedicated professionals, who shared their experience and expertise so unselfishly, this book could not have been written.

My office staff, medical colleagues, and friends tolerated with good humor the frenzy necessary for me to complete this book and remained unconditionally accepting of my intemperance and irascibility throughout the project.

Nadia Ramzy, Ph.D., a talented anthropologist and psychoanalyst, provided considerable insight into the links between culture and the borderline personality. Barbara Linder, M.Ed., a psychiatric counselor on the CTU, and her patients, generously donated audio tapes of group sessions, which allowed us to capture a more visceral feeling for the healing process.

Craig Cuddeback of Cracom Corporation and the editors at HP Books/Price Stern Sloan expressed enthusiasm in our initial proposals and offered insight and guidance throughout the writing process. Jean Hohl helped type the manuscript and provided some valuable editorial suggestions.

Finally, we wish to thank our wives and children who supported us with their encouraging presence and spurred us on to tackle this project. They had to endure more than they bargained for in our writing of this book. We hope our efforts justify their forbearance.

Though all of these people were important contributors, it is our patients who ultimately teach us everything we know. They courageously share their lives and offer their trust, which we can only hope to justify. They are the people, most of all, who make this book possible and are the final arbiters of its worth.

Grateful acknowledgment is made for permission to reprint excerpts from:

"Your Inner Child of the Past" by W. Hugh Missildine, © 1963 by W. Hugh Missildine, reprinted by permission of Simon & Schuster, Inc.

"Marilyn, A Biography" by Norman Mailer, © 1973 by Alskog, Inc., and Norman Mailer, reprinted by permission of the author and the author's agent, Scott Meredith Literary Agency, Inc., 845 Third Avenue, New York, NY 10022.

"Marilyn" by Gloria Steinem, © by East Toledo Productions, reprinted by permission of Henry Holt & Company, Inc.

"The Culture of Narcissism" by Christopher Lasch, © 1978 by W.W. Norton & Company, Inc., reprinted by permission of W.W. Norton & Company, Inc.

"Thomas Wolfe, A Biography" by E. Nowell, © 1960, reprinted by permission of Doubleday, a division of Bantam, Doubleday, Dell Publishing Group.

"Diagnostic and Statistical Manual of Mental Disorders," Third Edition, © 1987 by the American Psychiatric Association, reprinted by permission of the American Psychiatric Association.

Contents

Contents

Preface

For decades, physicians treated diseases and illnesses as the symptoms occurred, with little attention to prevention. The idea of preventing heart attacks and strokes, for example, by implementing certain lifestyle changes—diet, exercise, nicotine/drug abstinence—was almost completely unheard of. Aside from a few basic home remedies, self-care was viewed only as a poor second choice to prescribed medications and treatments.

In general, patients relied on the medical profession to correct their condition rather than prevent it. They did not expect thorough explanations of diseases, nor did doctors provide them as part of their professional services. Basically, the public viewed illnesses as numbers on a roulette wheel—one was lucky and stayed healthy or one became sick or injured and went to a doctor for treatment.

This approach has changed radically over the past thirty years. Self-care and preventive medicine have become central components of quality health care programs. Medical research, consumer awareness, and dramatically rising health care costs have led to a recognition that many diseases can be prevented with proper preventive measures. More than ever, people are concerned about their health; they want to understand and take control of it.

This trend has also been apparent in the area of mental health. Clinicians are making concerted efforts to educate patients on the origins and treatment of specific disorders. The American Psychiatric Association (APA) and other professional groups are much more active in promoting legislation and increasing general awareness of mental illness. Consumer organizations, such as the National Alliance for the Mentally Ill (NAMI), are disseminating educational pamphlets and offering hot line services to help patients and their families cope with various forms of mental illness.

Yet, despite this general trend, people are rarely given the opportunity to read about mental illness in easily understandable language. Countless times in my practice I have been asked by patients and their families for reading material on Borderline Personality Disorder (BPD)—the focus of this book. Each time, I have had to mutter apologies about the lack of published material for the layperson.

Perhaps the most exacting price we've had to pay for an uninformed populace is the continued and unfair social stigma attached to mental illness. Physical illnesses are rarely blamed on the victim. In the popular vernacular, one typically "comes down with," "is afflicted by," or "contracts" a certain physical disease; blame is typically attributed to some form of environmental condition or microorganism.

Not so in the case of many mental disorders. The general perception is that one "is" or "becomes" manic-depressive, neurotic, schizophrenic, or borderline; the implication is subtle, but inescapable—the victim shoulders much of the blame. While this may be true in some cases, in many cases it is not. Regardless, this perception has, in general, fostered misunderstanding, antagonism, and uneasiness about the mentally ill. People who would not think twice about visiting a friend in a hospital, for example, may dread—or feel extremely embarassed about—visiting the same friend in a psychiatric hospital. People who seem to understand complex explanations of physical diseases cannot fathom the origins or behaviors associated with mental disorders. In many ways, our understanding of mental illness has not caught up to our understanding of physical illness; our empathy for the victims is certainly light years behind. Though this situation is certainly unfortunate, it is also quite predictable: Psychology wasn't really deemed a science until around the turn-of-the century, and still today the physiological complexity of the human mind remains one of life's greatest mysteries.

Our lack of understanding has also resulted in a high societal price tag: lack of adequate public funding for mental health facilities, frequent abuses of the mentally ill, and the myriad of violent acts associated with mental illness—wife and child abuse, incest, alcohol- and drug-related crimes, to name only a few. The number of the severely mentally ill keep increasing, yet the facilities for treating these people are actually decreasing. Ultimately, the financial and moral costs for cleaning up the "toxic waste" that spill from the inadequate treatment of the mentally ill are enormous.

Due to an information lag, a gap has formed between the myths concerning BPD and accurate, widely disseminated information on its causes and treatment. Though BPD afflicts an estimated 10 million Americans, very few people in the general population could even vaguely describe the disorder. There are many reasons for this—the relative newness of the diagnosis, its controversial standing among some members of the mental health profession, and, perhaps most importantly, the elusive, inconsistent, contradictory nature of the disorder itself.

Yet despite these factors BPD involves some of our most vital social issues—child abuse, poor quality day care, destruction of the nuclear family, divorce, geographical mobility, the changing roles of women. In addition, borderline personality offers a new context in which to view some of our most baffling, yet increasingly widespread, psychological maladies—bulimia, anorexia nervosa, alcohol and drug abuse, depression, and suicide.

In fact, many in the mental health profession believe that we are living in a "borderline era." Just as the hysterical neurotic of Freud's time represented the repressive European culture of the early twentieth century, the borderline's fragmented sense of identity and difficulty in maintaining stable relationships may reflect the fragmentation of stable units in contemporary society.

This book seeks to fill the present information gap on Borderline Personality Disorder; as such, it is intended for general audiences who simply want to know more about this widespread and disturbing syndrome. But we have tried to do more than merely inform: We have tried to explore the syndrome in such a way that the reader can understand intellectually—and feel emotionally—what it is like to be a borderline personality. From the identification with this kind of subjective experience, we believe, springs true understanding.

Loneliness, fear of abandonment, impulsive self-destructiveness, storminess in relationships, inability to achieve intimacy—these are feelings that we all experience at one time or another. The borderline personality, however, lives with these feelings almost constantly and experiences them to a much higher degree. Many people are in great mental and emotional pain—pain that can be just as searing and perhaps even more frightening than physical pain—and do not know why or what to do about it or how to seek help. Those readers who have been diagnosed with the syndrome, or are considering therapy, will find explanatory material unburdened (when at all possible) by complex psychiatric jargon. Hopefully, this book will lead to self-knowledge, provide comfort, reassurance, and coping strategies, and offer some practical options for therapy not heretofore available.

We have also identified certain aspects of contemporary society that increasingly foster borderline characteristics and we suggest some directions for change.

Though the book is geared for a general lay audience, professionals should also find it a great help. It may be used not only as a reference but also as recommended reading for patients and clients who are hungry for knowledge about BPD. The wide-ranging symptomology of BPD given in this book should apply to the work of psychiatrists, clinical and research psychologists (particularly those focusing on child development), psychotherapists and family therapists, substance abuse counselors, pastoral counselors, eating disorder specialists, stress consultants, and others. The Appendices—covering DSM-III-R classifications and medications used for treatment of borderline personality disorders, the evolution of borderline personality disorder in psychoanalytic thought and other theories of borderline personality—should be particularly appealing to the professional.

We hope this book provides families and friends of borderlines with workable strategies for coping with this most distressing illness. Borderline Personality Disorder is generally recognized as one of the most frustrating psychiatric conditions to live with and to treat. Yet, diagnostically and practically, the borderline is defined by the nature of his past and present relationships with others. We believe this essential human interdependency, when properly directed, can be used as a tool that can help the borderline and those closest to him or her. We hope this book will make the trip easier.

1

The World of the Borderline

"Everything looked and sounded unreal. Nothing was what it is. That's what I wanted—to be alone with myself in another world where truth is untrue and life can hide from itself."

—*From* A Long Day's Journey Into Night *by Eugene O'Neill*

DR. WHITE THOUGHT it would all be relatively straightforward. Over the five years he had been treating Jennifer, she had few medical problems. Her stomach complaints were probably due to gastritis, he thought, so he treated her with antacids. But when her stomach pains became more intense despite treatment and routine testing proved normal, Dr. White admitted Jennifer to the hospital.

After a thorough medical work-up, Dr. White inquired about stresses Jennifer might be experiencing at work and home. She readily acknowledged that her job as a personnel manager for a major corporation was very pressured, but as she put it, "Many people have pressure jobs." She also revealed that her home life was more hectic recently: She was trying to cope with her husband's busy legal practice while tending to the responsibilities of being a mother. But she doubted the connection of these factors to her stomach pains.

When Dr. White recommended that Jennifer seek psychiatric consultation, initially she resisted. It was only after her discomfort turned into stabs of pain that she reluctantly agreed to see the psychiatrist, Dr. Gray.

They met a few days later. Jennifer was an attractive blonde woman who appeared younger than her twenty-eight years. She lay in bed in a hospital room that had been transformed from an anonymous cubicle into a personalized lair. A stuffed animal sat next to her in bed and another lay on the night stand beside several pictures of her husband and son. Get well cards were meticulously displayed in a line along the window sill, flanked by flower arrangements.

At first, Jennifer was very formal, answering all of Dr. Gray's questions with great seriousness. Then she joked about how her job was "driving me to see a shrink." The longer she talked, the sadder she looked. Her voice became less authoritative and more childlike.

She told him how a job promotion was exacting more demands—duties about which she felt unsure. Her five-year-old son was starting school, which was proving to be a difficult separation for both of them. Conflicts with Allan, her husband, were increasing. She described rapid mood swings and trouble sleeping. Her appetite had steadily decreased and she was losing weight. Her concentration, energy, and sex drive had all diminished.

Dr. Gray recommended a trial of antidepressant medications, which improved her gastric symptoms and seemed to normalize her sleeping patterns. In a few days she was ready for discharge and agreed to continue outpatient therapy.

Over the following weeks, Jennifer talked more about her upbringing. Reared in a small town, she was the daughter of a prominent businessman and his socialite wife. Her father, an elder in the local church, demanded perfection from his daughter and her two older brothers, constantly reminding the children that the community scrutinized their behavior. Jennifer's grades, her behavior, even her thoughts were never quite good enough. She feared her father, yet constantly—and unsuccessfully—sought his approval. Her mother remained passive and detached. Her parents evaluated her friends, often deeming them unacceptable. As a result, she had few friends and even fewer dates.

Jennifer described her roller-coaster emotions, which seemed to have worsened when she started college. She began drinking for the first time, sometimes to excess. Without warning, she would feel lonely and depressed and then high with happiness and love. On occasion, she would burst out in rage against her friends—fits of anger that she had somehow managed to suppress as a child.

It was about this time that she also began to appreciate the attention of men, something she had previously always avoided. Though she enjoyed being desired, she always felt she was "fooling" or tricking them somehow. After she began dating a man, she would sabotage the relationship by stirring up conflict.

She met Allan as he was completing his law studies. He pursued her relentlessly and refused to be driven away when she tried to back off. He liked to choose her clothes and advise her on how to walk, how to talk, and how to eat nutritiously. He insisted she accompany him to the gym where he frequently worked out.

"Allan gave me an identity," she explained. He advised her on how to interact with other lawyers, when to be aggressive, when to be demure. She developed a cast of "repertoire players" whom she could call on stage on cue.

They married, at Allan's insistence, before the end of her junior year. She quit school and began working as a receptionist, but her employer recognized her intelligence and promoted her to more responsible jobs.

At home, however, things began to sour. Allan's career and his interest in body-building caused him to spend more time away from home, which Jennifer hated. Sometimes she would start fights just to keep him home a little longer. Occasionally she provoked him into hitting her. Afterward she would invite him to make love to her.

Jennifer had few friends. She devalued women as gossipy and uninteresting. She hoped that Scott's birth, coming two years after her marriage, would provide the comfort she lacked. She felt her son would always love her and always be there for her. But the demands of an infant were overwhelming, and after a while, Jennifer decided to return to work.

Despite frequent praise and successes at work, Jennifer continued to feel insecure, that she was "faking it." She became sexually involved with a co-worker, who was almost forty years her senior.

"Usually I'm okay," she told Dr. Gray. "But there's another side that takes over and controls me. I'm a good mother. But my other side makes me a whore; it makes me act crazy!"

Jennifer continued to deride herself, particularly when alone; during times of solitude, she would feel abandoned, which she attributed to her own unworthiness. Anxiety would threaten to overwhelm her unless she found some kind of release. Sometimes she'd indulge in eating binges, once consuming an entire bowl of cookie batter. She would spend long hours gazing at pictures of her son and husband, trying to "keep them alive in my brain."

Jennifer's physical appearance at her therapy sessions fluctuated dramatically. When coming directly from work, she would dress in a business suit that exuded maturity and sophistication. But on days off she showed up in short pants and knee socks, with her hair in braids; at these appointments she acted like a little girl with a high-pitched voice and a limited vocabulary.

Sometimes she would transform right before Dr. Gray's eyes. She could be insightful and intelligent, working collaboratively toward greater self-understanding, and then become a child, coquettish and seductive, pronouncing herself incapable of functioning in the adult world. She could be charming and ingratiating or manipulative and hostile. She could storm out of one session, vowing never to return, and at the next session cower with the fear that Dr. Gray would refuse to see her again.

Jennifer felt like a child clad in the armor of an adult. She was perplexed at the respect she received from other adults; she expected them to see through her disguise at any moment, revealing her as an emperor with no clothes. She needed someone to love and protect her from the world. She desperately sought closeness, but when someone came too close, she ran.

Jennifer is afflicted with Borderline Personality Disorder (BPD). She is not alone. Recent studies estimate that 10 million or more Americans may be affected by BPD.[1,2] Between 15 and 25 percent of all patients seeking psychiatric care are diagnosed with the disorder, and it is by far the most common of all personality disorders.[3]

Yet despite its prevalence, BPD remains virtually unknown to the general public. Ask the man-on-the-street about anxiety, depression, or alcoholism, and he would probably be able to provide a sketchy, if not technically accurate, description of the illness. Ask him to define Borderline Personality Disorder, and he would probably give you a blank stare. For more than a decade, BPD has been lurking as a kind of "Third World" of mental illness—indistinct, massive, vaguely threatening.

BPD has been underpublicized partly because the diagnosis is so new. For years, "borderline" was used as a catch-all category for patients who did not fit more established diagnoses. People described as "borderline" seemed more ill than neurotics (who experience severe anxiety secondary to emotional conflict), yet less ill than psychotics (whose detachment from reality makes normal functioning impossible.)

The disorder also appeared to coexist with, and border on, other mental illnesses: hysteria, manic-depressive disorder, schizophrenia, hypochondriasis, multiple personality disorder, sociopathy, alcoholism, eating disorders, phobias, and obsessive compulsive disorders.

Psychiatrists could not seem to agree on the separate existence of the syndrome, much less on the specific symptoms necessary for diagnosis. Even today, studies corroborate that about 90 percent of patients with the BPD diagnosis also share at least one other psychiatric diagnosis.[4]

In many ways, the borderline syndrome has been to psychiatry what the virus is to general medicine: an inexact term for a vague but pernicious illness that is frustrating to treat, difficult to define, and impossible for the doctor to explain adequately to his patient.

Though the term *borderline* was first coined in the 1930s, the condition was not clearly defined until the 1970s. As more and more people began to seek therapy for a unique set of life problems, the parameters of the disorder crystallized. In 1980, Borderline Personality Disorder was included in the American Psychiatric Association's third edition of *The Diagnostic and Statistical Manual* (DSM III), the diagnostic "bible" of the psychiatric profession. (The revised DSM-III-R, published in 1987, further refines the diagnosis.) Though various schools within psychiatry still quarrel over the exact nature, causes, and treatment of BPD, the disorder is officially recognized as a major mental health problem in America today.

DEMOGRAPHIC BORDERS

Who are the borderline people one meets in everyday life? She is Carol, a friend since grade school. Over a minor slight, she accuses you of stabbing her in the back and tells you that you were really never her friend at all. Weeks or months later, Carol calls back, congenial and blasé, as if nothing had happened between you.

He is Bob, a boss in your office. One day, Bob bestows glowing praise on your efforts in a routine assignment; another day he berates you for an insignificant error. At times he is reserved and distant; other times he is suddenly and uproariously "one of the boys."

She is Arlene, your son's girlfriend. One week, she is the picture of preppy; the next, she is the epitome of punk. She breaks up with your son one night, only to return hours later, pledging endless devotion.

He is Brett, your next door neighbor. Unable to come to grips with his collapsing marriage, he denies his wife's obvious unfaithfulness in one breath, and then takes complete blame for it in the next. He clings desperately to his family, caroming from guilt and self-loathing to raging attacks on his wife and children who have so "unfairly" accused him.

If the people in these short profiles seem inconsistent, it should not be surprising—inconsistency is the hallmark of BPD. Unable to tolerate paradox, borderlines are walking paradoxes, human Catch-22s. Their inconstancy is a major reason why the mental health profession has had such difficulty defining a uniform set of criteria for the illness.

If these people seem all too familiar, this also should not be surprising. The chances are good that you have a spouse, relative, close friend, or coworker who is borderline. Perhaps you know a little bit about BPD or recognize borderline characteristics within yourself.

Though it is difficult to get a firm grasp on the figures, mental health professionals generally agree that the number of borderlines in the general population is growing—and at a rapid pace—though some observers claim that it is the therapists' awareness of the disorder that is growing rather than the number of borderlines.

Is borderline personality really a modern-day "plague," or is merely the diagnostic label *borderline* new? In any event, the disorder has provided new insight into the psychological framework of several related conditions. Numerous studies have linked BPD with anorexia, bulimia, drug addiction, and teenage suicide—all of which have increased alarmingly over the last decade. Some studies have uncovered BPD in approximately 50 percent of all patients who have eating disorders.[5] Other studies have found that over 50 percent of substance abusers also fulfill criteria for BPD.[67]

Self-destructive tendencies or suicidal gestures are very common among borderlines—indeed, they are one of the syndrome's defining criteria. The incidence of documented death by suicide is about 8 to 10 percent among borderlines and even higher for borderline adolescents. A history of previous suicide attempts, a chaotic family life, and a lack of support systems increase the likelihood. The risk multiplies even more among borderline patients who also suffer from depressive or manic-depressive disorders, or from alcoholism or drug abuse.[8]

EMOTIONAL HEMOPHILIA

DSM-III-R lists eight criteria for BPD, five of which must be present for diagnosis.[9] At first glance, these criteria may seem unconnected or only peripherally related. When explored in-depth, however, the eight symptoms are seen to be intricately connected, interacting with each other so that one symptom sparks the rise of another like the pistons of a combustion engine.

The eight criteria may be summarized as follows (each is described in-depth in Chapter 2):

(1) Unstable and intense interpersonal relationships.
(2) Impulsiveness in potentially self-damaging behaviors, such as substance abuse, sex, shoplifting, reckless driving, binge eating.
(3) Severe mood shifts.
(4) Frequent and inappropriate displays of anger.
(5) Recurrent suicidal threats or gestures, or self-mutilating behaviors.
(6) Lack of clear sense of identity.

(7) Chronic feelings of emptiness or boredom.
(8) Frantic efforts to avoid real or imagined abandonment.

Beneath the clinical nomenclature lies the anguish experienced by borderlines and their families and friends. For the borderline, much of life is a relentless emotional roller coaster with no apparent destination. For those living with, loving, or treating the borderline, the trip can seem just as hopeless and frustrating.

Jennifer and millions of other borderlines are provoked to rage uncontrollably against the people they love most. They feel helpless and empty, dissipating their identity.

Mood changes come swiftly, explosively, carrying the borderline from the heights of joy to the depths of depression. Filled with anger one hour, calm the next, he often has little inkling about why he was driven to such wrath. Afterward, the inability to understand the origins of the episode brings on more self-hate and depression.

A borderline suffers a kind of emotional hemophilia; he lacks the clotting mechanism needed to moderate his spurts of feeling. Stimulate a passion, and the borderline emotionally bleeds to death.

Sustained periods of contentment are foreign to the borderline. Chronic emptiness eats at him until he is forced to do anything in order to escape. In the grip of these lows, the borderline is prone to a myriad of impulsive, self-destructive acts—drug and alcohol binges, eating marathons, anorexic fasts, bulimic purges, gambling forays, shopping sprees, sexual promiscuity, and self-mutilation. He may attempt suicide, often not with the intent to die but to feel *something*, to confirm he is alive.

"I hate the way I feel," confesses one borderline. "When I think about suicide, it seems so tempting, so inviting. Sometimes, it's the only thing I relate to. It is difficult not to want to hurt myself. It's like, if I hurt myself, the fear and pain will go away."

Central to the borderline syndrome is the lack of a core sense of identity. When describing themselves, borderlines typically paint a confused or contradictory self-portrait, in contrast to neurotic patients who have a much clearer sense of who they are. To overcome their indistinct and mostly negative self-image, borderlines, like actors, are constantly searching for "good roles," complete "characters" they can use to fill the identity void. So they often adapt like chameleons to the environment, situation, or companions of the moment, much like the title character in Woody Allen's film, *Zelig*, who literally assumes the personality, identity, and appearance of anyone around him.

The lure of ecstatic experiences, whether attained through sex, drugs, or other means, is sometimes overwhelming for the borderline personality. In ecstasy, he can return to a primal world where the self and the external world merge—a form of second infancy. During periods of intense loneliness and emptiness, the borderline will go on drug binges, bouts with alcohol, sexual escapades (with one or several partners), sometimes lasting days at a time. It is as if when the struggle to find identity becomes intolerable, the answer is either to lose identity altogether or to achieve a semblance of self through pain or numbness.

The family background of a borderline is often marked by alcoholism, depression, and emotional disturbances. A borderline childhood is often a desolate battlefield, scarred with the debris of indifferent, rejecting, or absent parents, emotional deprivation, and chronic abuse. One study reported that a history of verbal, physical, and/or sexual abuse, or of prolonged separation or neglect by primary caregivers was the most important factor in distinguishing borderline patients from those with other disorders.[10] Other studies have found a history of severe psychological, physical, or sexual abuse in 20 to 75 percent of borderline patients.[10, 11]

These unstable relationships carry over into adolescence and adulthood, where romantic attachments are highly charged and usually short-lived. The borderline will frantically pursue a man (or woman) one day and send him packing the next. Longer romances—usually measured in weeks or months rather than years—are usually filled with turbulence and rage, wonder, and excitement.

SPLITTING: THE BLACK-AND-WHITE WORLD OF THE BORDERLINE

The world of a borderline, like that of a child, is split into heroes and villains. A child emotionally, the borderline cannot tolerate human inconsistencies and ambiguities; he cannot reconcile another's good and bad qualities into a constant coherent understanding of that person. At any particular moment, one is either "good" or "evil" there is no in-between, no gray area. Nuances and shadings are grasped with great difficulty, if at all. Lovers and mates, mothers and fathers, siblings, friends, and psychotherapists may be idolized one day, totally devalued and dismissed the next.

When the idealized person finally disappoints (as we all do, sooner or later), the borderline must drastically restructure his one-dimensional conceptualization. Either the idol is banished to the dungeon, or the borderline banishes himself in order to preserve the "all-good" image of the other person.

This type of behavior, called "splitting," is the primary defense mechanism employed by the borderline. Technically defined, splitting is the rigid separation of positive and negative thoughts and feelings about oneself and others, that is, the inability to synthesize these feelings. Normal persons are ambivalent and can experience two contradictory feeling states at one time; borderlines characteristically shift back and forth, entirely unaware of one feeling state while in another.

Splitting creates an escape hatch from anxiety: The borderline typically experiences a close friend or relation (call him "Joe") as two separate people at different times. One day, she can admire "Good Joe" without reservation, perceiving him as completely good; his negative qualities do not exist; they have been purged and attributed to "Bad Joe." Other days, she can guiltlessly and totally despise "Bad Joe" and rage at his badness without self-reproach—for now his positive traits do not exist; he fully deserves the rage.

Intended to shield the borderline from a barrage of contradictory feelings and images—and from the anxiety of trying to reconcile those images—the splitting mechanism often achieves quite the opposite effect: The frays in the personality fabric become full-fledged rips; the sense of his own identity and the identities of others shifts even more dramatically and frequently.

STORMY RELATIONSHIPS

Though feeling continually victimized by others, a borderline ironically and desperately seeks out new relationships, for solitude, even temporary aloneness, is more intolerable than mistreatment. To escape the loneliness, the borderline will flee to singles bars, the arms of recent pick-ups, somewhere—anywhere—to meet someone who might save her from the torment of her own thoughts, much like Theresa Dunn in Judith Rossner's *Looking for Mr. Goodbar*.

In the relentless search for a structured role in life, the borderline is typically attracted to—and attracts to her—others with complementary personality disorders. The domineering, narcissistic personality of Jennifer's husband, for example, cast her in a role with little effort. He was able to give her an identity even if the identity involved submissiveness and mistreatment.

Yet, for a borderline, relationships often disintegrate quickly. Maintaining closeness with a borderline requires an understanding of the syndrome and a willingness to endure a long walk on a perilous tightrope. Too much closeness threatens the borderline with suffocation. Keeping one's distance or leaving a borderline alone—even for brief periods—recalls the sense of abandonment he felt as a child. In either case, the borderline reacts intensely.

In a sense, the borderline carries only a sketchy map of interpersonal relations; he finds it extremely difficult to gauge the optimal psychic distance from others, particularly significant others. To compensate, he caroms back and forth from clinging dependency to angry manipulation, from outpourings of gratitude to irrational hate. He fears abandonment, so he clings; he fears engulfment, so he pushes away. He craves intimacy and is terrified of it at the same time. He winds up repelling those with whom he most wants to connect.

JOB PROBLEMS

Though borderlines have extreme difficulties managing their personal lives, many are able to function productively in a work situation—particularly if the job is well-structured, clearly defined, and supportive. Many perform well for long periods, but then suddenly—because of a change in the job structure, or a drastic shift in personal life, or just plain boredom and a craving for change—they abruptly leave or sabotage their position and go on to the next opportunity.

The work world can provide sanctuary from the anarchic

setting of social relationships. For this reason, borderlines frequently function best in highly structured work environments. The helping professions—medicine, nursing, clergy, counseling—also attract many borderlines who strive to achieve the power or control that elude them in social relationships. In these roles borderlines provide the care for others that they yearn for in their own lives.

Borderlines are often very intelligent and display striking artistic abilities; fueled by easy access to powerful emotions, they can be creative and successful.

But a highly competitive or unstructured job, or a highly critical supervisor, can trigger the intense, uncontrolled anger and the hypersensitivity to rejection to which the borderline is susceptible. The rage can permeate the work place and literally destroy a career.

A "WOMAN'S ILLNESS"?

Recent estimates indicate that women borderlines outnumber men by two to one among outpatients and perhaps by as much as four to one among hospitalized patients.[3] Why do women seem so much more vulnerable to BPD than men? Some researchers propose that the same constitutional-hereditary factors that predispose women to affective (mood) disorders are responsible for their vulnerability to BPD. Since some doctors feel BPD is closely associated with affective disorders, and affective disorders are more common in women, then BPD would be more frequently observed in females.[12]

Another theory is that the separation-individuation phase between mother and infant is more difficult for girls, resulting in more identity problems later in life.[13] Many theoreticians point to the influence of social factors on women, particularly women's shifting role patterns over the past twenty-five years (see Chapter 4).[14]

Though the statistics are quite straightforward, some critics dispute their reliability, pointing out that women are more likely to enter therapy than men, so are more likely to be diagnosed as borderline.[14] Other critics feel that a kind of clinician bias operates with borderline diagnoses: Psychotherapists perceive problems with identity as more "normal" in men; as a result, they may underdiagnose BPD among men.[15]

Still other researchers believe that just as many men fulfill borderline criteria as women, but whereas women tend to become depressed, attempt suicide, or seek psychiatric care, men tend to act out violently against the world. The effect of not being able to regulate emotion in females leads to internalized, self-directed violence; the same problem in males results in aggressive and antisocial behavior. Eventually, the males are diagnosed as sociopathic and are channeled through the criminal justice system, where they may elude correct diagnosis forever.

BPD IN DIFFERENT AGE GROUPS

Many of the features of the borderline syndrome—impulsivity, tumultuous relationships, identity confusion, mood instability—are major developmental problems for the adolescent. Indeed, establishing a core identity is the primary quest for both the teenager and the borderline. It follows, then, that BPD is diagnosed more commonly among adolescents and young adults than other age groups.[16]

Early investigations of BPD among the elderly led to the impression that the syndrome was rare in this age group. Some researchers hypothesized that older borderline adults were able to achieve stabilization over time; or, at least, they reached a point where they were no longer distressed enough to seek out further medical care.

More recently, however, BPD has been increasingly recognized among the elderly, challenging the presumption that borderlines "mature out" over time. On the other hand, this observation may also be a function of the increased interest in older populations who have often been neglected in research studies in the past.[16][17][18]

Older adults must contend with a progressive decline in physical and mental functioning, which can be a perilous adaptive process for the aging borderline. For the fragile identity, the task of altering expectations and adjusting self-image can exacerbate symptoms. The aging borderline may deny deteriorating functions, project the blame for deficiencies onto others, and become increasingly paranoid; at other times, he may exaggerate handicaps and become more dependent.

SOCIOECONOMIC FACTORS

Borderline pathology has been identified in about equal proportions in all cultures and economic classes in the United States. However, the consequences of poverty on infants and children—higher stress levels and lack of good child care, psychiatric care, and pregnancy care (perhaps resulting in brain insults or malnutrition)—might lead to higher incidence of BPD among the poor. Perhaps the poor have not been diagnosed borderline more often because they have less access to medical care or are less interested in obtaining psychiatric help.

GEOGRAPHIC BORDERS

Although most of the theoretical formulations and empirical studies of the borderline syndrome have been conducted in the United States, other countries—Canada, Mexico, Israel, Sweden, Denmark, other Western European nations and the USSR—have recognized borderline pathologies within their populations.

Comparative studies are scant at this point but could provide great insight into the childrearing, cultural, and social threads that compose the causal fabric of the syndrome.

BORDERLINE BEHAVIOR IN WELL-KNOWN PEOPLE AND FICTIONAL CHARACTERS

Whether the borderline personality is a new phenomenon, or simply a new label for an interrelated cluster of internal feelings and external behaviors, is a topic of considerable debate in the mental health community. Most psychiatrists believe that the borderline syndrome has been around for quite some time; that its increasing prominence results not so much from the mind of the patient but from the mind of the clinician. Indeed, many psychiatrists believe that some of Freud's most interesting cases of "neurosis" at the turn of the century would today be clearly diagnosed as borderline.[19]

Perceived in this way, the borderline syndrome becomes an interesting new perspective from which to understand some of our most complex personalities—both past and present, real and fictional. Conversely, well-known figures and characters can be used to illustrate different aspects of the syndrome. Along these lines, biographers and others have speculated that the term might apply to such wide ranging figures as Marilyn Monroe, Zelda Fitzgerald, Thomas Wolfe, T.E. Lawrence, Adolph Hitler, and Moamar Kadafi. Cultural critics can observe borderline features in Blanche Dubois in *A Streetcar Named Desire*; Martha in *Who's Afraid of Virginia Woolf?*; Sally Bowles in *Cabaret*; Travis Bickle in *Taxi Driver*; Howard Beale in *Network*; Carmen in Bizet's opera; and Terry Dunn in *Looking for Mr. Goodbar*.

THE QUESTION OF BORDERLINE "PATHOLOGY"

To one degree or another, we all struggle with the same issues as the borderline—the threat of separation, fear of rejection, confusion about identity, feelings of emptiness and boredom. How many of us have not had a few intense, unstable relationships? Or flew into a rage now and then? Or felt the allure of ecstatic states? Or dreaded being alone, or gone through mood changes, or been self-destructive in some way?

If nothing else, BPD serves to remind us that the line between "normal" and "pathological" may sometimes be a very thin one. Do we all display, to one degree or another, some symptoms of borderline personality? The answer is probably "Yes," but not all of us are controlled by the syndrome to the degree that it disrupts—or rules—our lives. With its extremes of emotion, thought, and behavior, BPD represents some of the best and worst of human character—and of our society in the waning years of the twentieth century. By exploring its depths and boundaries, we may be facing up to our ugliest instincts and our highest potentials—and the hard road we must travel to get from one point to the other.

2

Chaos and Emptiness

"All is caprice. They love without measure those whom they will soon hate without reason."
—*Thomas Sydenham, 17th-century English physician on "hystericks," the equivalent of today's borderline personality.*

"I SOMETIMES WONDER if I'm possessed by the devil," says Carrie, a social worker in the psychiatric unit of a large hospital. "I don't understand myself. All I know is, this borderline personality of mine has forced me into a life where I've cut everyone out. So it's very, very lonely."

Carrie was diagnosed with the borderline syndrome in 1983, after twenty-two years of therapy, medications, and hospitalizations for a variety of mental and physical illnesses. By then, her medical file resembled a well-worn passport, the pages stamped with the numerous psychiatric "territories" through which she had traveled.

"For years I was in and out of hospitals, but I never found a therapist who understood me and knew what I was going through."

Carrie's parents were divorced when she was an infant, and

she was raised by her alcoholic mother until she was nine. A boarding school took care of her for four years after that.

When she was twenty-one, overwhelming depression forced her to seek therapy; she was diagnosed and treated for depression at that time. A few years later, her moods began to fluctuate wildly and she was treated for bipolar disorder (manic-depression). Throughout this period she repeatedly overdosed on medications and cut her wrists many times.

"I was cutting myself and overdosing on tranquilizers, antidepressants, or whatever drug I happened to be on," she recalls. "It had become almost a way of life."

In her mid-twenties, she began to have auditory hallucinations and became severely paranoid. At this time she was hospitalized for the first time and diagnosed schizophrenic.

And still later in life, Carrie was hospitalized in a cardiac-care unit numerous times for severe chest pains, subsequently recognized to be anxiety-related. She went through periods of binge-eating and starvation-fasting; over a period of several weeks, her weight would vary by as much as seventy pounds.

When she was thirty-two, she was brutally raped by a physician on the staff of the hospital in which she worked. Soon after, she returned to school and was drawn into a sexual relationship with one of her female professors. By the age of forty-two, her collection of medical files was filled with almost every diagnosis imaginable, including schizophrenia, depression, bipolar disorder, hypochondriasis, anxiety, anorexia nervosa, sexual dysfunction, and post-traumatic stress disorder (following the rape).

Despite her mental and physical problems, Carrie was able to perform her work fairly well. Though she changed jobs frequently, she managed to complete a doctorate in social work. She was even able to teach for awhile at a small women's college.

Her personal relationships, however, were severely limited. "The only relationships I've had with men were ones in which I was sexually abused. A few men have wanted to marry me, but I have a big problem with getting close or being touched. I can't tolerate it. It makes me want to run. I was engaged a couple of times, but had to break them off. It's unrealistic of me to think I could be anybody's wife."

As for friends, she says, "I'm very self-absorbed. I say everything I think, feel, know, or don't know. It's so hard for me to get interested in other people."

After more than twenty years of treatment, Carrie's symptoms were finally recognized and diagnosed in 1983 as BPD. Her dysfunction evolved from ingrained, enduring personality traits, more indicative of a personality or "trait" disorder than her previously diagnosed, transient "state" illnesses.

"The most difficult part of being a borderline personality has been the emptiness, the loneliness, and the intensity of feelings," she says today. "The extreme behaviors keep me so confused. At times I don't know what I'm feeling or who I am."

A better understanding of Carrie's illness has led to more consistent treatment. Medications have been useful for treating acute symptoms and providing the glue for maintaining a more coherent sense of self; at the same time, she has acknowledged the limitations of the medications.

Her psychiatrist, working with her other physicians, has helped her to understand the connection between her physical complaints and her anxiety and to avoid unnecessary medical tests, drugs, and surgeries. Psychotherapy has been geared for the "long haul," focusing on her dependency and stablization of her identity and relationships, rather than on an endless succession of acute emergencies.

Carrie, at forty-six, has had to learn that an entire set of previous behaviors are no longer acceptable. "I don't have the option of cutting myself, or overdosing, or being hospitalized anymore. I vowed I would live in and deal with the real world, but I'll tell you, it's a frightening place. I'm not sure yet whether I can do it or whether I *want* to do it."

BORDERLINE: A PERSONALITY DISORDER

Carrie's journey through this maze of psychiatric and medical symptoms and diagnoses exemplifies the confusion and desperation experienced by individuals afflicted with mental illness and by those who minister to them. Though the specifics of Carrie's case might be considered extreme by some, thousands of women—and men—suffer similar problems with relationships, intimacy, depression, and drug abuse. Perhaps if she had been diagnosed earlier and more accurately, she could have been spared some of the pain and loneliness.

Though borderline personalities suffer a tangle of painful symptoms that severely disrupt their lives, only recently have psychiatrists begun to understand the disorder and treat it effectively. What is a "personality disorder?" What exactly does borderline border? How is borderline personality similar to and different from other disorders? How does the borderline syndrome fit into the overall schema of psychiatric medicine? These are difficult questions even for the professional, particularly in light of the elusive, paradoxical nature of the illness and its curious evolution in psychiatry.

As a personality disorder, BPD is distinguished by a cluster of longstanding, ingrained traits that are prominent in an individual's character. These traits are relatively inflexible and result in maladaptive patterns of perceiving, behaving, and relating to others.

BPD is one of eleven personality disorders noted in DSM-III-R. In DSM-III terminology, personality disorders are categorized on Axis II. (See Appendix A for a more detailed discussion of categorization in DSM-III-R.)

In contrast, state disorders (Axis I in DSM-III-R) are usually not as enduring as trait disorders. State disorders, such as depression, schizophrenia, anorexia nervosa, chemical dependency, are more often time- or episode-limited. Symptoms may emerge suddenly and then be resolved, as the patient returns to "normal." Many times these illnesses are directly correlated with imbalances in the body's physiology and can often be treated with medications, which virtually eliminate the symptoms.

Symptoms of a personality disorder, on the other hand, tend to be more durable traits and change only gradually; medications are, in general, less effective. Psychotherapy is primarily indicated, though other treatments, including medication, may alleviate some of the more acute symptoms, such as severe agitation or depression (see Chapter 7). Borderline and other personality disorders may be a secondary diagnosis, describing the underlying characterological functioning of a patient who exhibits more acute and prominent symptoms of a state disorder.

Comparisons to Other Disorders

Because the borderline syndrome often masquerades as a different illness and is often associated with other illnesses, clinicians often fail to recognize that BPD may be an important component in evaluating a patient. As a result, the borderline often becomes, like Carrie, a well-traveled patient, evaluated by multiple hospitals and doctors and accompanied throughout life by an assortment of diagnostic labels.

BPD can interface with other disorders in several ways. First, BPD can coexist with state (Axis I) disorders in such a way that borderline pathology is camouflaged. For example, BPD may be submerged in the wake of a more prominent and severe depression. After resolution of the depression with antidepressant medications, borderline characteristics may surface and only then be recognized as the underlying character structure requiring further treatment.

Second, BPD may be closely linked and perhaps even contribute to the development of another disorder. For example, the impulsivity, self-destructiveness, interpersonal difficulties, deflated self-image, and moodiness often exhibited by patients with substance abuse or eating disorders may be more reflective of BPD than the primary Axis I disorder. Although it could be argued that chronic abuse of alcohol could eventually alter personality characteristics in such a way that a borderline pattern could evolve secondarily, it seems more likely that underlying character pathology would develop first and lead to alcoholism.

The question of which is the chicken and which is the egg may be impossible to resolve, but the development of illnesses associated with BPD may represent a kind of psychological vulnerability to stress. Just as certain individuals may have genetic and biological vulnerabilities to physical diseases—heart attacks, cancers, gastrointestinal disorders, etc.—many may also have biologically determined propensities to psychiatric illnesses, particularly when stress is added to an underlying vulnerability to BPD. Thus, under stress, one borderline turns to drugs, another develops an eating disorder, still another becomes severely depressed.

Third, BPD may so completely mimic another disorder that the patient may be erroneously diagnosed with schizophrenia, hypochondriasis, bipolar disease, or other illnesses.

Comparison to Schizophrenia

Schizophrenic patients are usually much more severely impaired than borderlines and less capable of manipulating and relating to others. Both kinds of patients may experience agitated, psychotic episodes, but these are usually less consistent and less pervasive over time for borderlines. Schizophrenics are much more likely to grow accustomed to their hallucinations and delusions and are often less disturbed by them. Additionally, both may be destructive and self-mutilating. But where the borderline usually can function appropriately the schizophrenic is much more severely impaired socially.

Comparison to Affective Disorders (Bipolar and Depressive Disorders)

Episodes of depression or mania represent radical departures in functioning. Between mood swings, these individuals maintain relatively normal lives and can usually be treated effectively with medications. Borderlines, however, typically have difficulties in functioning (at least internally) even when not experiencing mood swings. When self-destructive, threatening suicide, hyperactive, or experiencing wide and rapid mood swings, the borderline may appear bipolar (manic-depressive), but these mood variations are much more transient and less predictable in the borderline.

BPD and Hypochondriasis

The borderline may focus on his physical ills, complaining loudly and dramatically to medical personnel and acquaintances, in order to maintain dependency realtionships with them. He may be considered merely a hypochondriac, while the underlying understanding of his problems go completely ignored.

BPD and Multiple Personality Disorder

Some psychiatrists consider multiple personality—a state disorder—a special type of BPD. [1,2,3] Both disorders share common symptoms—impulsivity, angry outbursts, disturbed relationships, marked mood changes, and a propensity for self-mutilation. Splitting is a primary defense mechanism in both illnesses. Several studies have shown a high prevalence of BPD in patients with multiple personality disorder—as high as 82 percent in one report. [4,5]

BPD and Post-Traumatic Stress Disorder

Post-traumatic stress disorder (PTSD) is a complex of symptoms that follow an extraordinarily severe traumatic event, such as a natural disaster or combat. It is characterized by intense fear, emotional re-experiencing of the event, nightmares, irritability, exaggerated startle response, and so on. One study found BPD pathology in half of the patients diagnosed with PTSD.[6]

BPD and Associated Personality Disorders

Many characteristics of BPD overlap with those of other personality disorders. For example, the dependent personality shares with the borderline the features of dependency, avoidance of being alone, and strained relationships. But the dependent personality lacks the self-destructiveness, anger, and mood swings of a borderline. Similarly, the schizotypal personality exhibits poor relations with others and difficulty in trusting, but is more eccentric and less self-destructive. Often a patient exhibits enough characteristics of two or more personality disorders to warrant diagnoses for each. For example, a patient may demonstrate characteristics that lead to diagnoses of both borderline personality disorder and obsessive compulsive personality disorder.

In DSM-III-R, BPD is grouped in a cluster of personality disorders that generally reflect dramatic, emotional, or erratic features. The others in this group are narcissistic, antisocial, and histrionic personality disorders, to which BPD is often compared.

Both borderlines and narcissists display hypersensitivity to criticism; failures or rejections can precipitate severe depression. Both exploit others; both demand almost constant attention. The narcissistic personality, however, usually functions at a higher level. He has an inflated sense of self-importance, displays disdain for others, and lacks even a semblance of empathy. In contrast, the borderline has a lower self-esteem and is highly dependent on others' reassurance. The borderline desperately clings to others and is usually more sensitive to their reactions.

Like the borderline, the antisocial personality exhibits impulsivity, poor tolerance of frustration, and manipulative relationships. The antisocial personality, however, lacks a sense of guilt or conscience; he is more detached and is not purposefully self-destructive.

The histrionic personality shares with the borderline tendencies of attention-seeking, manipulativeness, and shifting emotions. The histrionic, however, usually develops more stable roles and relationships. He is usually more flamboyant in speech and manner, and emotional reactions are exaggerated. Physical attractiveness is the histrionic's primary concern.

BPD and Substance Abuse

BPD and chemical abuse are frequently associated. Two studies found that between 13 and 56 percent of hospitalized chemical abusers were also diagnosed with BPD.[7,8] Alcohol or drugs might reflect self-punishing, angry, or impulsive behaviors, a craving for excitement, or a mechanism of coping with loneliness. Drug dependency may be a substitute for nurturing social relationships, a familiar, comforting way to stabilize or self-medicate fluctuating moods, or a way to establish some sense of belonging or self-identification. These possible explanations for the appeal of chemical abuse are also some of the defining criteria for BPD.

The Anorexic Borderline or the Borderline Anorexic?

Anorexia nervosa and bulimia have become major health problems in this country, especially among young women.[9] Eating disorders are fueled by a fundamental distaste for one's own body and a general disapproval of one's identity. The anorexic sees herself in absolute, black or white extremes—as either obese (which she always feels) or thin (which she feels she never completely achieves). Since she constantly feels out of control, she impulsively utilizes starvation or binging and purging to maintain an illusion of self-control. The similarity of this pattern to the borderline pattern has led many mental health professionals to infer a connection between the two. Some studies have uncovered BPD in almost 50 percent of patients who have eating disorders.[10] Many experts in the field feel the percentage is actually much higher.

BPD and Compulsive Behaviors

Certain compulsive or destructive behaviors may reflect borderline patterns. For example, a compulsive gambler may continue betting despite a shortage of funds. He may be seeking a thrill from a world that habitually leaves him bored, restless, and numb. Or the gambling may be an expression of impulsive self-punishment.

Shoplifters often steal items they do not need. Fifty percent of bulimics exhibit kleptomania, drug use, or promiscuity.[11] When these behaviors are governed by compulsion, they may represent a need to feel or a need to self-inflict pain.

Promiscuity often expresses a need for constant love and attention from others, in order to hold on to positive feelings about oneself. The borderline typically lacks consistent positive self-regard and requires continuous reassurance. A borderline woman, lacking in self-esteem, may perceive her physical attractiveness as her only asset and may require confirmation of her worth by engaging in frequent sexual encounters. Such involvements avoid the pain of being alone and provide artificial relationships she can totally control. Feeling desired can instill a sense of identity. When self-punishment becomes a prominent part of the psychodynamics, humiliation and masochistic perversions may enter the relationships. From this perspective, it is logical to speculate that many prostitutes and pornographic actors and models may be borderline.

Difficulties with relationships may result in private, ritualistic thinking and behaviors, often expressed as obsessions or compulsions. A borderline may develop specific phobias as he employs magical thinking to deal with fears; sexual perversions may evolve as a mechanism to approach intimacy.

Suicide Among Adolescents

Suicidal threats or behaviors is one of the criteria of BPD. The suicide rate among adolescents has more than doubled over the past twenty years and is now the second leading cause of death among fifteen to twenty-four-year-olds.[12][13] Most youths who commit suicide have a history of psychiatric illness, usually affective disorder, or substance abuse.[14] Although studies on adolescent suicide are limited, BPD may be a primary factor in prompting an alienated youth to "go over the edge" and complete the act of suicide.

Appeal of Cults

Because borderlines yearn for direction and acceptance, they may be attracted to strong leaders of disciplined groups. The cult can be very enticing since it provides instant and unconditional acceptance, automatic intimacy, and a paternalistic leader who will be readily idealized. The borderline can be very vulnerable to such a black and white world view in which "evil" is personified by the outside world and "good" is encompassed within the cult group.

CLINICAL DEFINITION OF BORDERLINE PERSONALITY DISORDER

The current official definition of borderline pathology is contained in the DSM-III-R diagnostic criteria of Borderline Personality Disorder.[15] This description, initially developed by John Gunderson and others, emphasizes descriptive, observable behavior.[16] As such, it is narrower than Otto Kernberg's (see appendix B), which pays more attention to causes and intrapsychic functioning.

The following criteria have been demonstrated to discriminate BPD from other illnesses 80 percent or more of the time.[17] The diagnosis of BPD is confirmed when at least five of the following eight criteria are present:

The Relentless Search for Mr./Ms. Right

Criterion 1. Unstable and intense interpersonal relationships, with marked shifts in attitudes toward others (from idealization to devaluation or from clinging dependency to isolation and avoidance), and prominent patterns of manipulation of others.

The borderline's unstable relationships are directly related to his intolerance of separation and fear of intimacy. The borderline is typically dependent, clinging, and idealizing until the lover, spouse, or friend repels or frustrates these needs; then the borderline caroms to the other extreme—devaluation, resistance to intimacy, and outright avoidance. A continual tug-of-war develops between the wish to merge and be taken care of on the one hand, and the fear of engulfment on the other. For the borderline, engulfment means the obliteration of separate identity, the loss of autonomy, and a sense of feeling nonexistent. The borderline vacillates between wishes for closeness to relieve the emptiness and boredom, and fears of intimacy, which is perceived as the thief of self-confidence and independence.

In relationships, these internal feelings are dramatically translated into intense, shifting, manipulative couplings. The borderline often makes unrealistic demands of others, appearing to observers as spoiled. Manipulativeness is manifested through physical complaints and hypochondriasis, expressions of weakness and helplessness, provocative actions, and masochistic behaviors. Suicidal threats or gestures are often used to obtain attention and rescue (see criterion 5). The borderline may use seduction as a manipulative strategy, even with someone known to be inappropriate and inaccessible, such as a therapist or minister.

Though very sensitive to others, the borderline lacks true empathy. He may be dismayed to encounter an acquaintance, such as teacher, co-worker, or therapist, outside of his usual place of business because it is difficult to conceive of that person as having a separate life. Furthermore, he may not understand or be extremely jealous of his therapist's separate life, or even of other patients he may encounter.

The borderline lacks "object constancy," the ability to understand others as complex human beings who nonetheless can relate in consistent ways. The borderline experiences another on the basis of his most recent encounter, rather than on a broader-based, consistent series of interactions. Therefore, a constant, predictable perception of another person never emerges, as the borderline continues to respond to that person as someone new on each occasion.

Because of the borderline's inability to see the big picture, to learn from previous mistakes and to observe patterns in his own behavior, he often repeats destructive relationships. A female borderline, for example, will typically return to her abusive ex-husband, who proceeds to abuse her again; a male borderline frequently couples with similar, inappropriate women with whom he repeats sadomasochistic affiliations.

The borderline's endless quest is to find a perfect caregiver who will be all-giving and omnipresent. The search often leads to partners with complementary pathology; both lack insight into their mutual destructiveness. For example, Michelle desperately craves protection and comfort from a man. Mark displays a bravura self-assurance; even though the self-assurance covers a deep insecurity, it fits the bill for Michelle. Just as Michelle needs Mark to be her protective white knight, so Mark

needs Michelle to remain helpless and dependent on his be-
neficence. After a while, both fail to live up to their assigned
stereotypes. Mark cannot bear the narcissistic wounds of challenge or failure and begins to cover his frustrations with alcohol
and by physically abusing Michelle. Michelle bristles under his
controlling yoke, yet becomes frightened when she sees his
weaknesses. The dissatisfactions lead to more provocation and
more conflict.

Afflicted with self-loathing, the borderline distrusts others'
expressions of caring. Sam, for example, was a twenty-one-year-
old college student whose chief complaint in therapy was "I
need a date." An attractive man with serious interpersonal problems, Sam characteristically approached inaccessible women.
Whenever his overtures were accepted, he immediately devalued the woman as no longer desirable.

All of these characteristics make it difficult for borderlines to
achieve real intimacy. As Carrie relates, "A few men have
wanted to marry me, but I have a big problem with getting close
or being touched. I can't tolerate it." The borderline cannot seem
to gain enough independence to be dependent in healthy, rather
than desperate, ways. True sharing is sacrificed to a demanding
dependency and a desperate need to join with another person in
order to complete one's own identity, as kind of Siamese twins
of the soul.

The Impulsive Character

Criterion 2. Impulsiveness in at least two areas that are potentially self-destructive, e.g., chemical abuse, sexual promiscuity,
gambling, shoplifting, excessive spending, overeating, anorexia
nervosa, or bulimia.

The borderline's behaviors may be sudden and contradictory
since they typically result from strong, momentary feelings—
perceptions that represent isolated, unconnected snapshots of
experience. The immediacy of the present exists in isolation,
without the benefit of the experience of the past, or the hopeful-
ness of the future. Because historical patterns, consistency, and
predictability are unavailable to the borderline, similar mistakes
are repeated again and again.

The borderline is in the ironic yet untenable position of achieving what an entire generation strove for in the 1960s—"living in the now." For the borderline, there is no escape from the "now," if even for brief respite and perspective. Reality is, as Octavio Paz calls it, "an endless instant": "a staircase going neither up or down, we don't move, today is today, always is today."[18]

The borderline's limited patience and need for immediate gratification may be connected to behaviors that define other BPD criteria: Impulsive conflict and rage may emerge from the frustrations of a stormy relationship (criterion 1); precipitous mood changes (criterion 3) may result in impulsive outbursts; inappropriate outbursts of anger (criterion 4) may develop from a failure to control impulses; self-destructive or self-mutilating behaviors (criterion 5) may result from the borderline's frustrations. Often, impulsive actions such as drug and alcohol abuse serve as defenses against feelings of loneliness and abandonment.

Joyce was a thirty-one-year-old divorced woman who increasingly turned to alcohol after her divorce and her husband's subsequent remarriage. Though attractive and talented, she let her work deteriorate and spent more time at bars. "I made a career out of avoiding," she later said. When the pain of being alone and feeling abandoned became too great, she would use alcohol as anesthesia. She would sometimes pick up men and take them home with her. Characteristically, after such alcohol or sexual binges, she would berate herself with guilt and feel deserving of her husband's abandonment. Then the cycle would start again, as she required more punishment for her worthlessness. Thus, self-destructiveness became both a means of avoiding pain and a mechanism for inflicting it as expiation for her sins.

Radical Mood Shifts

Criterion 3. Affective instability: marked shifts from baseline mood to depression, irritability, or anxiety, usually lasting a few hours and only rarely more than a few days.

The borderline undergoes abrupt mood shifts, lasting for short periods—usually hours. His base mood is not usually calm and controlled, but more often either hyperactive and irrepressible or pessimistic, cynical, and depressed.

Thomas Wolfe, one of America's great novelists, often bounced between periods of energetic creativity and boundless enthusiasm to periods of morbid self-pity, unproductivity, and depression, when he would project blame for his failures onto others.

At one point while working prodigiously on his writings, he experienced morbid melancholia. At that time he was traveling in Europe, separated from his wife.

> Today has been a horrible one. I was able to sleep only the most diseased and distressed sleep, the worst sort of American in Europe sleep and I got sick with the shakes, the day was the most horrible European sort, something that passes understanding. The wet, heavy air that deadens the soul, puts a lump of indigestible lead in the solar plexus, depresses and fatigues the flesh until one seems to lift himself leadenly through the thick, wet, steaming air. With this terrible kind of fear, an excitement that is without hope, that awaits only the news of some further grief, failure or humiliation and torture. A lassitude that enters the soul and makes one hope for better things and better work tomorrow but hope without belief and conviction.[19]

Raging Bull

Criterion 4. Inappropriate, intense anger, or lack of control of anger, e.g., frequent displays of temper, constant anger, recurrent physical fights.

The borderline's outbursts of rage are as unpredictable as they are frightening. Violent scenes are disproportionate to the frustrations that trigger them. Domestic fracases that may involve chases with butcher knives and thrown dishes are typical of borderline rage. The anger may be sparked by a particular (and often trivial) offense, but underneath the spark lies an arsenal of fear from the threat of disappointment and abandonment.

The rage, so intense and so near the surface, is often directed at the borderline's closest relationships—spouse, children, parents. Borderline anger may represent a cry for help, a testing of devotion, or a fear of intimacy—whatever the underlying factors, it pushes away those whom the borderline needs most. The spouse, friend, lover, or family member who sticks around despite these assaults may be very patient and understanding or, sometimes, very disturbed himself. In the face of these eruptions, empathy is difficult and the relation must draw on every resource at hand in order to cope (see Chapter 8).

The rage often carries over to the therapeutic setting, where psychiatrists and other mental health professionals become the target. Carrie, for example, often raged against her therapist, constantly looking for ways to test his commitment to staying with her in therapy. Treatment becomes precarious in this situation (see Chapter 7) and many therapists have been forced to drop borderline patients for this reason. Most therapists will, whenever possible, try to limit the number of borderline patients they treat.

Pleas for Help

Criterion 5. Recurrent suicidal threats, gestures, or behavior, or self-mutilating behaviors.

Suicidal threats and gestures—reflecting both the borderline's propensity for overwhelming depression and hopelessness, and his knack for manipulating others—are prominent features of BPD. Often, the frequent threats or half-hearted suicide attempts are not a wish to die but rather a way to communicate pain and a plea for others to intervene. Unfortunately, when habitually repeated, these suicidal gestures often lead to just the opposite scenario—others get fed up and stop responding, which may result in progressively more serious attempts. Suicidal behavior is one of the most difficult BPD symptoms for family and therapists to cope with: Addressing it can result in endless unproductive confrontations; ignoring it can result in death (see Chapters 6-8).

Self-mutilation—except when clearly associated with psychosis—is the hallmark of BPD. This behavior, more closely connected to BPD than any other psychiatric malady, may take the form of self-inflicted wounds to the genitals, limbs, or torso. For these borderlines, the body becomes a road map highlighted with self-inflicted scars. Razors, scissors, fingernails, and lit cigarettes are some of the more common instruments used; excessive use of drugs, alcohol, or food can also inflict the damage.

Often, self-mutilation begins as an impulsive, self-punishing action, but over time it may become a studied, ritualistic procedure. In such instances the borderline may carefully scar body areas that are covered by clothing—which illustrates the borderline's intense ambivalence: He feels compelled to flamboyantly self-punish, yet he carefully conceals the evidence of his tribulation.

Jennifer (see Chapter 1) would fulfill her need to self-inflict pain by scratching her wrists, abdomen, and waist, leaving deep fingernail marks that could easily be covered.

Sometimes the self-punishment is more indirect. The borderline may often be the victim of recurrent "quasi-accidents." He may provoke frequent fights. In these incidents, the borderline feels less directly responsible; circumstances or others provide the violence for him.

When Harry, for example, broke up with his girlfriend, he blamed his parents. They had not been supportive enough or friendly enough, he thought, and when she ended the affair after six years, he was forlorn. At twenty-eight he continued to live in an apartment paid for by his parents, and worked sporadically in his father's office. Earlier in his life he had attempted suicide but decided he wouldn't give his parents "the satisfaction" of killing himself. Instead he engaged in increasingly dangerous behaviors. He had numerous automobile accidents, some while intoxicated, and continued to drive despite the revocation of his driver's license. He frequented bars where he sometimes picked fights with men much bigger than he. Harry recognized the destructiveness of his behavior and sometimes wished that "one of these times I would just die."

These dramatic self-destructive behaviors and threats may be explained in several ways. The self-inflicted pain may reflect the borderline's need to feel, to escape an encapsulating numbness. Borderlines form a kind of insulating bubble that not only protects them from emotional hurt but also serves as a barrier from the sensations of reality. The experience of pain, then, becomes an important link to existence. Often, however, the inflicted pain is not strong enough to transcend this barrier (though the blood and scars may be fascinating for the borderline to observe), in which case the frustration may compel him to accelerate attempts to induce pain.

Self-induced pain can also function as a distraction from other forms of suffering. One patient, when feeling lonely or afraid, would cut different parts of her body as a way "to take my mind off" the loneliness. Another would bang her head in the throes of stress-related migraine headaches.

Self-damaging behavior can also serve as an expiation for sin. One man, guilt-ridden after the breakup of his marriage for which he totally blamed himself, would repeatedly drink gin—a taste he abhorred—until reaching the point of retching. Only after enduring this discomfort and humiliation would he feel redeemed and able to return to his usual routine.

Painful, self-destructive behavior may be employed in an attempt to constrict actions that are felt to be dangerously out of control. One adolescent boy cut his hands and penis to dissuade himself from masturbation, an act he considered loathsome. He hoped that the memory of the pain would prevent him from further indulging in this repugnant behavior.

Impulsive, self-destructive acts (or threats) may result from a wish to punish another person, often a close relation. One woman consistently described her promiscuous behavior (often involving masochistic, degrading rituals) to her boyfriend. These affairs invariably occurred when she was angry and wanted to punish him.

Finally, self-destructive behavior can also evolve from a manipulative need for sympathy or rescue. One woman, after arguments with her boyfriend, repeatedly slashed her wrists in his presence, forcing him to secure medical assistance for her.

Many borderlines deny feeling pain during self-mutilation and even report a calm euphoria after it. Before hurting themselves, they may experience great tension, anger, or overwhelming sadness; afterwards there is a sensation of release and relief from anxiety.

This relief may result from psychological or physiological factors, or a combination of both. Physicians have long recognized that following severe physical trauma, such as battle wounds, the patient may experience an unexpected calm and a kind of natural anesthesia despite the lack of medical attention. Some have hypothesized that during such times, the body releases biological substances, such as endorphins, which serve as the organism's self-treatment of pain.

Who Am I?

Criterion 6. Marked and persistent identity disturbance manifested by uncertainty in at least two of the following: self-image, sexual orientation, long-term goals or career choice, type of friends desired, preferred values.

Borderlines lack a constant, core sense of identity, just as they lack a constant core conceptualization of others. The borderline does not accept her own intelligence, attractiveness, or sensitivity as constant traits, but rather as comparative qualities to be continually re-earned and judged against others'. The borderline may view herself as intelligent, for example, based solely on the results of a just-administered IQ test. Tomorrow, when she makes a "dumb mistake," she will revert to seeing herself as "stupid." The borderline considers herself attractive until she spies a woman whom she feels is prettier; then, she feels ugly again.

For the borderline, identity is graded on a curve. Who she is (and what she does) today determines her worth, with little regard to what has come before. The borderline allows herself no laurels on which to rest. Like Sisyphus, she is doomed to roll the boulder repeatedly up the hill, needing to prove herself over and over again. Self-esteem is only attained through impressing others; so pleasing others becomes critical to loving herself.

In *Marilyn*, Norman Mailer describes how Marilyn Monroe's search for identity became Marilyn's driving force, absorbing all aspects of her life:

> What an obsession is identity! We search for it, because the private sensation when we are in our own identity is that we feel sincere as we speak, we feel *real*, and this little phenomenon of good feeling conceals an existential mystery as important to psychology as the *cogito ergo sum*—it is nothing less than that the emotional condition of feeling real is, for whatever reason, so far superior to the feeling of a void in oneself that it can become for protagonists like Marilyn a motivation more powerful than the instinct of sex, or the hunger for position or money. Some will give up love or security before they dare to lose the comfort of identity.[20]

Later, Marilyn found sustenance in acting, particularly in "the Method":

Actors in the Method will *act out*; their technique is designed, like psychoanalysis itself, to release emotional lava, and thereby enable the actor to become acquainted with his depths, then possess them enough to become possessed by his role. A magical transaction. We can think of Marlon Brando in "A Streetcar Named Desire." To be possessed by a role is *satori* (or intuitive illumination) for an actor because one's identity can feel whole so long as one is living in the role.[21]

The borderline's struggle in establishing a consistent identity is related to a prevailing sense of inauthenticity—a constant sense of "faking it." Most of us experience this sensation at various times in our lives. When one starts a new job, for example, one tries to exude an air of knowledge and confidence. After gaining experience, the confidence becomes increasingly genuine because one has learned the system and no longer needs to fake it. As Kurt Vonnegut says, "We are what we pretend to be."

The borderline never reaches that point. He continues to feel like he is faking it and is terrified that he will, sooner or later, be "found out." This is particularly true when the borderline achieves some kind of success—it feels misplaced, undeserved.

This chronic sense of nongenuineness probably originates in childhood. As explored in Chapter 3, the preborderline often grows up feeling inauthentic due to various environmental circumstances—suffering physical or sexual abuse, being forced to adopt an adult's role while still a child or to parent his own sick parent. At the other extreme, he may be discouraged from maturing and separating, and be trapped in a dependent child's role well past an appropriate time for separation. In all of these situations, the borderline never develops a separate sense of self, but continues to "fake" a role which is prescribed by someone else. If he fails in the role, he fears he will be punished; if he succeeds, he is sure he will be uncovered as a fraud and be humiliated.

Unrealistic attempts at achieving a state of perfection are often part of the borderline pattern. For example, a borderline anorexic might try to maintain a constant low weight and become horrified if it varies as little as one pound, unaware that this expectation is unrealistic. Perceiving themselves as static, rather than in a dynamic state of change, borderlines may view any variation from this inflexible self-image as shattering.

Conversely, the borderline may search for satisfaction in the opposite direction—by frequently changing jobs, careers, goals, friends, sometimes even gender. By altering external situations and making drastic changes in lifestyle, he hopes to achieve inner contentment. Some instances of so-called "mid-life crisis" or "male menopause" represent an extreme attempt to ward off fears of mortality or deal with disappointments in life choices. An adolescent borderline may constantly change his clique of friends—from "jocks" to "burnouts" to "brains" to "geeks"— hoping to achieve a sense of belonging and acceptance. Even sexual identity can be a source of confusion for the borderline. Some writers have noted an increased incidence of homosexuality, bisexuality, and sexual perversions among borderline personalities.[2]

Cult groups that promise unconditional acceptance, a structured social framework, and a circumscribed identity are powerful attractions for the borderline personality. When the individual's identity and value system merge with the accepting group's, the group's leader assumes extraordinary power—to the point where he can induce followers to emulate his actions, even if fatal, as witnessed by the Jonestown Massacre in 1978.

Aaron, after dropping out of college, attempted to assuage his feelings of aimlessness by joining the Moonies. He left the cult after two years, only to return after two more years of directionless wandering among different cities and jobs. Ten months later, he left the group again, but this time, lacking a stable set of goals or a comfortable sense of who he was or what he wanted, he attempted suicide.

The phenomenon of "cluster suicides," especially among teenagers, may reflect weaknesses in identity formation. The national suicide rate dramatically leaps upward after the suicide of a famous person, such as Marilyn Monroe or Freddie Prinze. The same dynamics may operate among adolescents with fragile identity structures: They are susceptible to the suicidal tendencies of the peer group leader or of another suicidal teenage group in the same region.

Always Half Empty

Criterion 7. Chronic feelings of emptiness or boredom.

Lacking a core sense of identity, borderlines commonly experience a painful loneliness that motivates them to search for ways to fill up the "holes." The reports of many borderlines are akin to the almost physical sensation that Graham Greene describes in *A Sort of Life*: "Boredom seemed to swell like a balloon inside the head; it became a pressure inside the skull; sometimes I feared this balloon would burst and I would lose my reason."[23]

Many writers, of course, have labeled emptiness and boredom as the quintessential problems of the twentieth century and no attempt will be made here to go into the psychological ramifications. Suffice it to say that, for the borderline, the search for a way to relieve the boredom usually results in impulsive ventures into destructive acts and disappointing relationships. In many ways, the borderline seeks out a new relationship or experience not for its positive aspects but to escape the feeling of emptiness, acting out the existential destinies of characters described by Sartre, Camus, and other philosophers.

The borderline frequently experiences a kind of existential angst. This can be a major obstacle in treatment for it saps the motivational energy to get well. From this feeling state radiate many of the other features of BPD. Suicide may appear to be the only rational response to a perpetual state of emptiness. The need to fill the void or relieve the boredom can lead to outbursts of anger, self-damaging impulsiveness, especially drug abuse, and mood swings designed to elicit sensations of feeling.

"Others Act Upon me, Therefore I Am"

Criterion 8. Frantic efforts to avoid real or imagined abandonment.

Just as an infant cannot distinguish between the temporary absence of her mother and her "extinction," the borderline often experiences temporary aloneness as perpetual isolation. As a result, the borderline becomes severely depressed over the real or perceived abandonment by significant others and then enraged at the world (or whoever is handy) for depriving her of this basic fulfillment.

Particularly when they are alone, borderlines may lose the sensation of existing, of feeling real. Rather than embracing Descartes' "I think, therefore I am" principle of existence, they live by a philosophy closer to "Others act upon me, therefore I am."

The theologian Paul Tillich wrote that "loneliness can be conquered only by those who can bear solitude." Because the borderline finds solitude so difficult to tolerate, she is trapped in a relentless metaphysical loneliness from which the only relief comes in the form of the physical presence of others. So she will often rush to singles bars or other crowded haunts, much like Theresa Dunn in *Looking for Mr. Goodbar*, often with similar disappointing—or even violent—results.

In *Marilyn: An Untold Story*, Norman Rosten recalled Marilyn Monroe's hatred of being alone. Without people constantly around her, she would fall into a void, "endless and terrifying."[a]

Lee Strasberg, also a close friend and noted acting teacher, would spend hours with Marilyn, giving her the nurturing she had missed as a child. Her difficulty sleeping led to frequent bouts with drugs, and Strasberg would try to help her sleep without drugs, according to Gloria Steinem in *Marilyn*. "She wanted to be held. Not to be made love to but just supported, because when she'd taken the pills they'd somehow react on her so that she would want more. We wouldn't give them to her. That's why she got in the habit of coming over and staying over. I'd hold her a little and she'd go to sleep."[b]

Toward the end of her life, Marilyn felt "unimportant and insignificant," according to her last psychiatrist, Dr. Ralph Greenson. "The main mechanism she used to bring some feeling of stability and significance to her life was the attractiveness of her body."

When her body started to go, when another man she looked to as a father figure abandoned her, when she failed to have a child, when she was criticized, rejected, or blamed in her professional life, Marilyn's world caved in. She was "found out." She was only Norma Jean again, vulnerable to the massive depression and hopelessness that persona, or more closely lack of persona, meant to her. By most biographers' count, she attempted suicide at least three times and had numerous other close calls with death before finally succeeding.

For most of us, solitude is longed for, cherished, a rare opportunity to reflect on memories and matters important to our well-being—a chance to get back in touch with ourselves, to rediscover who we are: "The walls of an empty room are mirrors that double and redouble our sense of ourselves," John Updike writes in *The Centaur*.

But the borderline, with only the weakest sense of self, looks back at only vacant reflections. Aloneness recapitulates the panic that he experienced as a child when faced with the prospect of abandonment by parents: Who will take care of me? The pain of loneliness can only be relieved by the rescue of a fantasized lover, as expressed in the lyrics of countless love songs.

In addition to these eight criteria defining BPD, a ninth criterion—brief psychotic experiences—has been proposed by Gunderson. DSM-III-R, however, does not yet accept this criterion because of controversy over its frequency and its overlap with psychotic illnesses. The borderline may become transiently psychotic when confronted with stressful or very unstructured situations. For example, psychiatrists sometimes observe episodes of psychosis during classical psychoanalyis, which relies heavily on free association and uncovering past trauma in an unstructured setting. Psychosis may also be stimulated by illicit drug use. Unlike patients with psychotic illnesses, such as schizophrenia, mania, psychotic depression, or organic/drug illnesses, borderline psychosis is usually of shorter duration and perceived as more acutely frightening to the patient and extremely different from his ordinary experience. The most common psychotic experiences for the borderline involve feelings of unreality and paranoid delusions.

Just as DSM-III-R modified some of the language and features of BPD standardized in DSM-III, so we can expect future diagnostic refinements to evolve, particularly as more clinical and clinical and statistical research is done. Perhaps future formulations will include more psychodynamic features, such as the defense mechanisms that Kernberg emphasizes in his formulations of Borderline Personality Organization (see appendix B).

The borderline personality is clearly becoming acknowledged by mental health professionals as one of the most common psychiatric maladies in this country. The professional must be able to recognize the features of BPD to treat effectively large numbers of patients. The layperson must be able to recognize them to better understand those with whom he shares his life.

3

Roots of the Borderline Syndrome

"All happy families resemble one another; every unhappy family is unhappy in its own fashion."
—*From* Anna Karenina *by Leo Tolstoi*

GROWING UP WAS not easy for Dixie Anderson. Her father was rarely at home and when he was, he didn't say much. For years, she didn't even know what he did for a living, just that he was gone all the time. Margaret, Dixie's mother, called him a "workaholic." Throughout her childhood, Dixie sensed that her mother was hiding something, though Dixie was never quite sure what it was.

But when Dixie turned eleven, things changed. She was an "early developer," her mother said, but Dixie really wasn't sure what that meant. All she knew was that her father was suddenly home more than he had ever been and he was also more attentive. Dixie enjoyed the new attention and the new feeling of power she had over him when he was finished touching her. After he was done, he would do whatever she asked him.

About this same time, Dixie suddenly became more popular in the family's suburban neighborhood. The kids began to offer her their secret stashes of pot, and a few years later acid, coke, and angel dust.

Junior high school was a drag. Halfway through a school day, she'd wind up fighting with some of the other kids. She didn't care. She was tough; she had friends and drugs; she was cool. Once, she even punched her science teacher, whom she felt was a real jerk. He went to the principal, who expelled her.

At age thirteen she saw her first psychiatrist, who diagnosed her as hyperactive and treated her with several medications. She decided to run away. She packed an overnight bag, took a bus to the interstate, stuck out her thumb, and in a few minutes was on her way to Las Vegas.

The way Margaret saw it, no matter what she did, it always seemed to turn out the same with Dixie: Her older daughter could not be pleased. Dixie was so much like her husband Roger, always criticizing the way Margaret looked and the way she kept the house. She had tried everything to lose weight, amphetamines, booze, even the stomach operation; yet nothing seemed to work. She'd always been fat, always would be.

She often wondered why Roger married her. He was a handsome man; from the beginning she could not understand why he wanted her. After awhile it was obvious he didn't want her. He simply stopped coming home at night.

Dixie was the one bright spot in Margaret's life. Her other daughter, Julie, was already obese at age five and seemed a lost cause. But Margaret would do anything for Dixie. She clung to her daughter like a lifeline. But the more Margaret clung, the more Dixie resented it. She became more demanding, throwing tantrums, and screaming about her mother's weight. The doctors could do nothing to help Margaret; they said she was manic-depressive and addicted to alcohol and amphetamines. The last time she was in the hospital they gave her electroshock treatment. And now with Roger gone and Dixie always running away, the world was closing in.

Los Angeles was the same story as Las Vegas for Dixie: She was promised cars and money and good times. Well, she had ridden in a lot of cars, but the good times were few and far between. Her friends were losers and sometimes she had to sleep with a guy to "borrow" a few bucks. Finally, with nothing but a few dollars in her jeans, she went back home.

Dixie arrived to find Roger gone and her mother in a thick fog of depression and drug-induced numbness. In all this bleakness at home, it wasn't long before she fell back into her alcohol and drug habits. At fifteen she had been hopitalized twice for chemical abuse and was treated by a number of therapists. At sixteen, she became pregnant by a man she had met only a few weeks before. She married him soon after the pregnancy tests.

Seven months later, when Kim was born, the marriage began to fall apart. Dixie's husband was a weak and passive oaf who could not get his own life together, much less provide a solid home environment for their child.

By the time the baby was six months old, the marriage was over, and Dixie and Kim moved in with Margaret. It was then that Dixie became obsessed with her weight. She would go entire days without eating, and then eat frantically and voluminously only to vomit it all up in the toilet. What she couldn't get rid of by vomiting she eliminated in other ways: She ate squares of Ex-Lax as if they were candy. She exercised until sweat drenched her clothes and she was too exhausted to move. The pounds dropped off—but so did her health and her mood. Her periods stopped; her energy waned; her capacity to concentrate weakened. She became very depressed about her life and for the first time suicide seemed like a real alternative.

Initially she felt safe and comfortable when she was readmitted to the hospital, but soon her old self returned. By the fourth day, she was trying to seduce her doctor; when he didn't respond, she threatened him with all sorts of retaliation. She demanded extra privileges and special attention from the nurses and refused to participate in unit activities.

As abruptly as she had gone into the hospital, she pronounced herself cured and demanded discharge two weeks after admission. Over the next year, she would be readmitted to the hospital several times. She would also see several psychotherapists, none of whom seemed to understand or know how to treat her dramatic mood shifts, her depression, her loneliness, her impulsiveness with men and drugs. She began to doubt that she could ever be happy.

It wasn't long before Margaret and Dixie were again fighting and screaming at each other. For Margaret it was like seeing herself growing up all over again and making the same mistakes. She couldn't bear to watch it any longer.

Margaret's father had been just like Roger, a lonely, unhappy man who had little to do with his family. Her mother ran the family much like Margaret ran hers. And just as Margaret clung to Dixie, so had her mother clung to Margaret, trying desperately to mold her every step of the way. Margaret was fed her mother's ideas and feelings—and enough food for a battalion. By the age of sixteen, she was grossly obese and taking large amounts of amphetamines prescribed by the family doctor to suppress her appetite. By the age of twenty, she was drinking alcohol and taking Fiorinal to bring her down from the amphetamines.

Margaret was never able to please her mother in spite of the constant struggle for control between the two. Neither could Margaret please her own daughter or husband. She had never been able to make anyone happy, she realized, not even herself. Yet she persisted in trying to please people who would not be pleased.

Now, with Roger gone and Dixie so sick, Margaret's life seemed to be falling apart. Dixie finally told her mother how Roger had sexually abused her. And before Roger left, he had bragged all about his women. Despite everything, Margaret still missed him. He was alone, she knew, just like she was.

It was time, Dixie recognized, to do something about the plight of this self-destructive family. Or at least herself anyway. A job would be the first priority, something to combat the relentless boredom. But she was nineteen years old with a two-year-old child and no husband, and she still hadn't graduated high school.

With characteristic compulsiveness, she flung herself into a high school equivalency program and received her diploma in a matter of months. Within days of obtaining her diploma, she was applying for loans and grants to attend college.

Margaret had begun to take care of Kim and in many ways, the arrangement looked like it might work: Raising Kim gave Margaret some meaning in her life, Kim had built-in child care, and Dixie had time for her new mission in life. But soon, the system showed cracks: Margaret sometimes got too drunk or depressed to be of any help. When this happened, Dixie had a simple solution: She would threaten to take Kim away from Margaret. Both the grandmother and granddaughter obviously needed each other desperately, so Dixie was able to totally control the household.

Through it all, Dixie still managed to find time for men,

though her frequent liaisons were usually of short duration. She seemed to follow a pattern: Whenever a man started to care for her, she became bored. Distant, older men—unavailable doctors, married acquaintances, professors—were her usual type, but she would drop them the instant they responded to her flirtations. The young men she did become involved with were all members of a church that was strictly opposed to premarital sex.

Dixie avoided women and had no female friends. She thought women were weak and uninteresting. Men, at least, had some substance. They were fools if they responded to her flirtations and hypocrites if they did not.

As time went on, the more Dixie succeeded in her studies, the more frightened she became. She could pursue a particular interest—school, a certain man—relentlessly, almost obsessively, but with each success her demands on herself escalated into unrealistic proportions. Despite good grades, she would explode in rage and threaten to kill herself when she performed below expectations on an exam.

At times like these, her mother would try to console her, but Margaret was also becoming preoccupied with suicide, and the roles often reversed. Mother and daughter were again shuffling in and out of the hospital trying to overcome depression and chemical abuse.

Like her mother and grandmother, Kim didn't know her father very well either. Sometimes he came to visit, sometimes she went to the house that he shared with his mother. He always seemed awkward around her.

With her mother detached and her grandmother ineffectual or preoccupied with her own problems, Kim took control of the household by the time she was four. She ignored Dixie, who responded by ignoring her. If Kim threw a tantrum, Margaret would cave in to her wishes.

The household was in an almost constant state of chaos. Sometimes both Margaret and Dixie would be in the hospital at the same time, Margaret for her drinking, Dixie for her bulimia. Kim would then go to her father's house, although he was unable to care for her and would have his mother tend to her.

On the surface, Kim seems oddly mature for a six-year-old, despite the chaos around her. To her, other kids are, "just kids," without her experience. She doesn't think her particular type of maturity is unusual at all: She has seen old photographs of her mother and grandmother when they were her age, and in the snapshots they have the same look.

ACROSS GENERATIONS

In many respects, the Andersons' saga is typical among borderline cases: The factors contributing to the borderline syndrome often transcend generations. The genealogy of BPD is often rife with deep and long lasting problems, including suicide, incest, drug abuse, violence, losses, and loneliness.

It has been observed that borderlines often have borderline mothers, who, in turn, have borderline mothers.[1] This hereditary predisposition of BPD prompts a number of questions, such as: How do borderline traits develop? How are they passed down through families? Are they, indeed, passed down at all?

In examining the roots of this illness, these questions resurrect the traditional "nature versus nurture" question. The two major theories on the causes of BPD—one emphasizing developmental (psychological) roots, the other constitutional (biological and genetic) origins—reflect the dilemma.

A third theoretical category, which focuses on the grander environmental and sociocultural factors, such as our fast-paced, fragmented societal structure, destruction of the nuclear family, increased divorce rates, increased reliance on nonparental daycare, greater geographical mobility, and changing patterns of women's roles, is also important (see Chapter 4). Though empirical research has yet to be conducted on these environmental elements, many professionals speculate that these factors would tend to increase the prevalence of BPD.

The available evidence points to no one definitive cause—or even type of cause—of BPD. Rather, a combination of early developmental, neurobiological, and social factors are probably responsible for the illness.

A WORD ABOUT RESEARCH DATA

Most studies on the development and transmission of psychiatric syndromes employ indirect means of investigation, that is, retrospective reviews, patients' reconstructions of past events, interviews with relatives, and so on. These methods are fraught with inaccuracies and obstacles that make their validity suspect. Longitudinal research—following and objectively evaluating identified subjects and their families prospectively over time—is a much more accurate approach. Unfortunately, such methods have not yet been widely used in BPD research due to the relatively recent congealing of the diagnosis and the tremendous expense, time, and manpower necessary for such work.

DEVELOPMENTAL ROOTS

Developmental theories on the causes of BPD focus on the delicate interactions between child and caregivers, especially during the first few years of life. The ages of eighteen to thirty months, when the child begins the struggle to gain autonomy, are particularly crucial. Some parents actively resist the child's move toward separation and insist instead on a controlled, exclusive, often suffocating symbiosis. At the other extreme, other parents offer only erratic parenting (or are absent) during much of the childraising period and so fail to provide sufficient attention to, and validation for, the child's feelings and experiences. Either extreme of parental behavior can eventuate in the child's failure to develop a positive, stable sense of self and may lead to a constant, intense need for attachment and chronic fears of abandonment.

In many cases the disturbed parent-child relationship takes the more severe form of early parental loss or prolonged, traumatic separation, or both. As with Dixie, many borderlines have an absent or psychologically disturbed father. Primary mother figures (who may sometimes be the father) tend to be erratic and depressed and have significant psychopathology themselves, usually BPD. The borderline's family background is frequently marked by incest, violence, and/or alcoholism. Many cases show an ongoing hostile or conflictual relationship between mother and preborderline child.

Object Relation Theory and Separation-Individuation in Infancy

Object relations theory, a model of infant development, emphasizes the significance of the child's interactions with his environment, as opposed to internal psychic instincts and biological drives unconnected to sensations outside himself. According to theory, the child's relationships with "objects" (people and things) in his environment determines his later functioning.

The primary object relations model for the early phases of infant development was created by Margaret Mahler and colleagues.[2] They postulated that the infant's first one to two months of life were characterized by an obliviousness to everything except himself (the autistic phase). During the next four or five months, designated the *symbiotic phase*, he begins to recognize others in his universe, not as separate beings, but as extensions of himself.

In the following *separation-individuation period* extending through ages two to three years, the child begins to separate and disengage from the primary caregiver and begins to establish a separate sense of self. Mahler and others consider the child's ability to navigate through this phase of development successfully to be crucial for later mental health.

During the entire separation-individuation period, the developing child begins to sketch out boundaries between self and others, a task complicated by two central conflicts—the desire for autonomy versus closeness and dependency needs, and fear of engulfment versus fear of abandonment.

A further complicating factor during this time is that the developing infant tends to perceive each individual in the environment as two separate personae. For example, when mother is comforting and sensitive, she is seen as "all good." When she is unavailable or unable to comfort and soothe, she is perceived as a separate, "all bad" mother. When she leaves his sight, the infant perceives her as annihilated, gone forever, and cries for her return to relieve the despair and panic. As the child develops, this normal "splitting" is replaced by a healthier integration of mother's good and bad traits, and separation anxiety is replaced by the knowledge that mother exists even when she is not physically present and will, in time, return—a phenomenon commonly known as *object constancy* (see below).

Mahler divides separation-individuation into four overlapping subphases.

Differentiation Phase (5-8 months). In this phase of development, the infant becomes aware of a world separate from mother. "Social smiling" begins—a reaction to the environment, but directed mostly at mother. Near the end of this phase, the infant displays the opposite side of this same response—"stranger anxiety"—the recognition of unfamiliar people in the environment.

If the relationship with mother is supportive and comforting, reactions to strangers are mainly characterized by curious wonder. If the relationship is unsupportive, anxiety is more prominent; the child begins to separate positive and negative emotions toward other people, relying on splitting to cope with these conflicting emotions.

Practicing Phase (8-16 months). The practicing phase is marked by the infant's increasing ability to move away from mother, first by crawling, then by walking. These short separations are punctuated by frequent reunions to "check in" and "refuel," behavior that demonstrates the child's first ambivalence toward his developing autonomy.

Rapprochement Phase (16-25 months). In the rapprochement phase, the child's expanding world sparks the recognition that he possesses an identity separate from those around him. Reunions with mother and the need for her approval shape the deepening realization that she and others are separate, real people. It is in the rapprochement phase, however, that both child and mother confront conflicts that will determine future vulnerability to the borderline syndrome.

The mother's role during this time is to encourage the child's experiments with individuation, yet simultaneously provide a constant, supportive, refueling reservoir. The normal two year old develops a strong bond with parents, but also learns to separate temporarily from them with sadness rather than with rage or tantrum. When reunited with the parent, the child is likely to feel happy as well as angry over the separation. The nurturing mother empathizes with the child and accepts the anger without retaliation. After many separations and reunions, the child develops an enduring sense of self, love and trust for parents, and a healthy ambivalence about others.

The mother of a preborderline, however, tends to respond to her child in a different way—either by pushing her child away prematurely and discouraging reunion (perhaps due to her own fear of closeness), or by insisting on a clinging symbiosis (perhaps due to her own fear of abandonment and need for intimacy). In either case, the child becomes burdened by intense fears of abandonment and/or engulfment that are mirrored back to him by mother's own fears.

As a result, the child never grows into an emotionally separate human being. Later in life, the borderline's inability to achieve intimacy in personal relationships reflects this infant stage. When an adult borderline confronts closeness, she may resurrect from childhood either the devastating feelings of abandonment that always followed her futile attempts at intimacy or the feeling of suffocation from mother's constant smothering. To defy such controls risks losing mother's love; to satisfy her risks losing oneself.

This fear of engulfment is well illustrated by T.E. Lawrence (*Lawrence of Arabia*) who at age thirty-eight writes about his fear of closeness to his overbearing mother: "I have a terror of her knowing anything about my feelings, or convictions, or way of life. If she knew, they would be damaged; violated; no longer mine."[3]

Object Constancy Phase (25-36 months). By the end of the second year of life, assuming the previous levels of development have progressed satisfactorily, the child enters the object constancy phase, wherein the child recognizes that the absence of mother (and other primary caregivers) does not automatically mean her annihilation. The child learns to tolerate ambivalence and frustration. The temporary nature of mother's anger is recognized. The child also begins to understand that his own rage will not destroy mother. He begins to appreciate the concept of unconditional love and acceptance and develops the capacity to share and to empathize. The child becomes more responsive to father and others in the environment. Self-image becomes more positive, despite the self-critical aspects of an emerging conscience.

Aiding the child in all these tasks are transitional objects—the familiar comforts (teddy bears, dolls, blankets) that represent mother and are carried everywhere by the child to help ease separations. The object's form, smell and texture are physical representations of the comforting mother. Transitional objects are one of the first compromises made by the developing child in negotiating the conflict between the need to establish autonomy and the need for dependency. Eventually, in normal development, the transitional object is abandoned when the child is able to internalize a permanent image of a soothing, protective mother figure.

Developmental theories propose that the borderline is never able to progress to this object constancy stage. Instead, the borderline is fixated at an earlier developmental phase, in which splitting and other defense mechanisms remain prominent.

Because they are locked into a continual struggle to achieve object constancy, trust, and a separate identity, adult border-lines continue to rely on transitional objects for soothing. One woman, for example, always carried in her purse a newspaper article that contained quotes from her psychiatrist. When she was under stress, she would take it out, calling it her "security blanket." Seeing her doctor's name in print reinforced his exist-ence and his continued interest and concern for her.

Ritualized, superstitious acts, when done in extremes, may represent borderline utilization of transitional objects. Although the ballplayer who wears the same socks or refuses to shave while in the midst of a hitting streak, for example, may be exhibiting borderline tendencies of relying on superstitious symbols to provide soothing and protection, it is only when such behaviors are repeated compulsively and inflexibly, and when they take on unrealistic proportions, that such a person crosses the border into the borderline syndrome.

Childhood Conflicts

The child's evolving sense of object constancy is consistently rechallenged as he progresses through developmental mile-stones. The toddler entranced by fairy tales filled with all-good and all-bad characters encounters numerous situations in which he uses splitting as a primary coping strategy. Though now trusting mother's permanent presence, the growing child must still contend with the fear of losing her love. The four-year-old who is scolded for being "bad" may feel threatened with the withdrawal of mother's love; he cannot yet conceive of the possibility that mother may be expressing her own frustrations quite apart from his own behavior, nor has he learned that mother can be angry and yet love him just as much at the same time.

Eventually, children are confronted with the separation anxi-ety of starting school. "School phobia" is neither a real phobia nor related exclusively to school itself, but instead represents the subtle interplay between the child's anxiety and the reactions of parents who may reinforce the child's clinging with their own ambivalence about the separation.

Adolescent Conflicts

Separation-individuation issues are repeated during adolescence, when questions of identity and closeness to others once again become vital concerns. During both the rapprochement phase of infancy and adolescence, the child's primary mode of relating is less acting than *re*acting to others, especially parents. While the two-year-old tries to elicit approval and admiration from parents by molding his identity to emulate caregivers, the adolescent tries to emulate peers or adopts behaviors that are consciously different—even opposite—from those of parents. In both stages, the child's behavior is based less on independently determined internal needs than on reacting to the significant people in the immediate environment. Behavior becomes a quest to discover identity rather than to reinforce an established one.

An insecure teenager may ruminate endlessly about her boyfriend in a "he loves me, he loves me not" fashion. Failure to integrate these positive and negative emotions and to establish a firm, consistent perception of others leads to continued splitting as a defense mechanism. The adolescent's failure to maintain object constancy results in later problems with sustaining consistent, trusting relationships, establishing a core sense of identity, and tolerating anxiety and frustration.

Often, entire families adopt a borderline system of interaction, with the family members' undifferentiated identities alternately merging with and separating from each other. Melanie, the adolescent daughter in one such family, closely identified with her chronically depressed mother, who felt abandoned by her philandering husband. With her husband often away from home and her other children of much younger age, the mother fastened onto her teenage daughter, relating intimate details of the unhappy marriage and invading the teenager's privacy with intrusive questions about her friends and activities. Melanie's feelings of responsibility for her mother's happiness interfered to the point where she could not attend to her own needs. She even selected a college nearby so she could continue to live at home. Eventually Melanie developed anorexia nervosa, which became her primary mechanism for feeling in control, independent and comforted.

Similarly, Melanie's mother felt responsible and guilty for her daughter's illness. The mother sought relief in extravagant spending sprees (which she concealed from her husband) and then covered the bills by stealing money from her daughter's bank account. Mother, father and daughter were trapped in a dysfunctional family swamp, which they were unwilling to confront and from which they were unable to escape. In such cases, treatment of the borderline may require treatment of the entire family (see Chapter 7).

Traumas

Major traumas—parental loss, neglect, rejection, physical or sexual abuse—during the early years of development can increase the probability of BPD in adolescence and adulthood. Indeed, case histories of borderline patients are typically desolate battlefields, scarred by broken homes, chronic abuse and emotional deprivation.

Norman Mailer describes the effect of an absent parent on Marilyn Monroe, who never knew her father. Though his absence would contribute to her emotional instability in later life, it would also ironically be one of the motivating forces in her career:

> Great actors usually discover they have a talent by first searching in desperation for an identity. It is no ordinary identity that will suit them, and no ordinary desperation can drive them. The force that propels a great actor in his youth is insane ambition. Illegitimacy and insanity are the godparents of the great actor. A child who is missing either parent is a study in the search for identity and quickly becomes a candidate for actor (since the most creative way to discover a new and possible identity is through the close fit of a role).[4]

Raised in an orphanage during many years of her early childhood, Marilyn had to learn to survive with a minimum of love and attention. It was her self-image that suffered the most and led to her manipulative behavior with lovers later in life:

One housemother for ten orphans—how can an institution afford more?—and yet what competition to get the
fragment of good feeling available in a woman who must
divide that small pie of her working heart into ten slices.
How little can be there, yet for the children what huge
and ruthless elbowing to get up under her nose for
reward, often by telling the most skillful lies, all the while
knowing the most complete loneliness if one is to the
rear. The real horror is that slowly, progressively, the
child loses all sense of inhabiting even the fair volume of
its own body.[5]

Throughout her life, Marilyn searched for a father to replace
the one she had never known. Marilyn's mother had kept a
photograph of Clark Gable on her bureau, a memory Marilyn
kept her whole life. In many ways, Clark Gable became her
"fantasy father."[6] When Gable, Marilyn's costar in *The Misfits*,
died shortly after production of the movie, it was an excruciating
loss.

Not all children who are traumatized or abused become borderline adults, of course; nor do all borderline adults have a
history of trauma or abuse. Further, most studies on the effects
of childhood trauma are based on inferences from adult reports
and not on longitudinal studies that follow young children
through to adulthood. Finally, other studies have demonstrated
less extreme forms of abuse in the histories of borderlines,
particularly neglect (sometimes from the father), and a rigid,
tight marital bond that excludes adequate protection and support for the child.[7,8,9] Nevertheless, the large amount of anecdotal
and statistical evidence demonstrates a link between various
forms of abuse, neglect, and BPD.

CONSTITUTIONAL FACTORS

Some psychiatrists believe that biological and genetic factors
play a crucial role in the development of borderline personality.
This viewpoint is supported by the fact that individuals vary
widely in their responses to poor childraising. Even many professionals who accept the importance of developmental influences also feel that some kind of biological predisposition is

probable. Though no specific biological or genetic markers, such as a blood test or an identifiable gene, have as yet been found, some research has yielded interesting results.

Biochemical Imbalances

Some theorists believe that BPD may result at least partly from biochemical imbalances, similar to those implicated in other psychiatric illnesses. These theories are supported by the fact that certain medications, including antidepressants, major tranquilizers and antiseizure medicines, have relieved disabling symptoms in some borderline patients (see appendix C). In most of these cases, however, it appears that despite improvements in the targeted symptoms, the underlying character pathology persists.

Recent studies have proposed a link between impulsive acts and abnormalities in the metabolism of serotonin, a chemical neurotransmitter implicated in mood disorders.[10] Researchers have suggested that the same impulsivity observed among borderlines (and perhaps bulimics and substance abusers) may be related to similar metabolic defects.[11]

The borderline's frequent abuse of food, alcohol and other drugs—typically interpreted as self-destructive behavior—may also be seen as an attempt to self-medicate inner emotional turmoil. Borderlines frequently report the calming effects of self-mutilation; rather than feeling pain, they experience soothing relief or distraction from internal psychological pain. Self-mutilation, like any other physical trauma or stress, may result in the release of endorphins—the body's natural narcotic-like substances that provide relief during childbirth, physical traumas, long-distance running, and other physically stressful activities.

Neurological Factors

BPD has been associated with certain neurological disorders, some of which may be inherited: learning disabilities, attention deficit disorder (hyperactivity), epilepsy, head trauma, and encephalitis. This link has been observed mostly among borderline adolescents.[12]

Some studies have revealed abnormal brainwave activity over the temporal lobe of borderline patients, suggesting possible dysfunction in this part of the brain. These researchers also found abnormally high levels of a pituitary hormone during tests.[13]

Studies have demonstrated that during sleep borderlines exhibit a distinctive brainwave activity known as short REM latency—an abbreviated time span preceding the onset of dreaming—a characteristic pattern documented in depressed patients. These patterns were present in most borderlines whether they were depressed or not.[14, 15, 16]

A Genetic Connection?

Psychiatrists frequently find that one or both parents of borderlines also display borderline characteristics. The fact that many borderline mothers have borderline children has long been known, but the inference has been that borderline personality has been transmitted through parent-child interaction rather than through genes.

Some genetic studies have confirmed that borderline patients have a higher than expected percentage of mood disorders, alcoholism and other personality disorders among blood relatives.[17, 18, 19] Debate continues on the genetic transmission of both schizophrenia and BPD.[20, 21, 22] Since many of these bordering disorders have themselves been linked to genetic factors, it stands to reason that BPD may also have genetic roots.

NATURE VERSUS NURTURE

The "nature-nurture" question is, of course, a long-standing and controversial one that applies to many aspects of human behavior. Is one afflicted with BPD because of a biological destiny inherited from parents—or because of the way parents handled—or mishandled—upbringing? Do the biochemical and neurological signs of the disorder cause the illness—or are they caused *by* the illness? Why do some people develop BPD in spite of an apparently healthy upbringing? Why do others, burdened with a background filled with trauma and abuse, not develop it?

These "chicken-or-egg" dilemmas can lead to false assumptions. For example, one might conclude, based on developmental theories, that the causal direction is strictly downward, that is, an aloof, detached mother would produce an insecure borderline child. But the relationship might be more complex, more interactive than that: A colicky, unresponsive, unattractive infant may generate disappointment and detachment in the mother. Regardless of which comes first, both continue to interact and perpetuate interpersonal patterns, which may endure over many years and extend to other relationships. The mitigating effects of other factors—a supportive father, accepting family and friends, superior education, physical and mental abilities—will help determine the ultimate emotional health of the individual.

Though no evidence supports a specific BPD gene, humans may inherit chromosomal vulnerabilities that are later expressed as a particular illness, depending on a variety of contributing factors—childhood frustrations and traumas, specific stress events in life, healthy nutrition, access to health care and so on. Just as some have postulated that inheritable biological defects in the body's metabolism of alcohol may be associated with an individual's propensity to alcoholism, so there may exist a genetic predisposition for BPD involving a biological weakness in stabilizing mood and impulses.

As many borderlines learn that they must reject the either-or, black-or-white ways of thinking, researchers are beginning to appreciate that the most likely model for BPD (and for most medical and psychiatric illnesses) recognizes multiple contributing factors—nature and nurture—working and interacting simultaneously. Borderline personality is a complex tapestry, richly embroidered with innumerable, intersecting threads.

4

The Borderline Society

"Where there is no vision, the people perish."
—*Proverbs. 29:18.*
"States are as the men are; they grow out of human characters."
—*From Plato's* Republic

FROM THE BEGINNING Lisa couldn't do anything right. Her older brother was the golden boy: good grades, respectful, athletic, perfect. Her younger sister, who had asthma, was also lavished with constant attention. Lisa was never good enough, especially in the eyes of her father. She remembered how he constantly reminded all of the children that he had started with nothing, that his parents had no money, didn't care about him, and drank too much. But he had prevailed. He had worked his way through high school, college, and even medical school. Now he was a well-respected surgeon, chairman of the department.

Lisa's earliest memories of her mother were of her lying on the couch either sick or in pain, ordering her about to clean house. Lisa tried hard to care for her mother and to convince her to stop taking the pain pills that seemed to make her so foggy.

Lisa felt that if she was just good enough, she could not only make her mother better but also please her father. Though her grades were always very good (even better than her brother's), her father always maligned her achievements: the course was too easy or she could have done even better. At one point, she thought she might want to become a doctor, but her father said she would never make it.

When her father drank too much, he became violent, sometimes hitting the kids harder than he intended. The most frightening time of all was when he was drunk and their mother was spaced out on pain pills; then there was no one to take care of them—except Lisa, and she hated it.

During those times she felt lost and isolated. It was similar to the way she felt in biology class when she'd look around the room and observe the other kids looking in the microscopes, taking notes, apparently knowing exactly what to do, while she experienced a queasy sensation in her stomach of not quite understanding what was expected of her, and feeling too frightened to ask for help.

After awhile she just stopped trying. In high school she began to hang out with the "wrong kids." She made sure her parents saw them and how freaky they dressed; she made sure they saw her kiss the Hispanic boy, whom they despised.

Because her father insisted she couldn't make it as a doctor, Lisa went into nursing. At her first hospital job, she met a "free spirit" who wanted to bring his nursing expertise to underprivileged areas. Lisa was enthralled by him and they married soon after meeting. His habitual, "social" drinking became more prominent as the months went by, and he began hitting her. Bruised and battered, Lisa still felt it was her fault—she just wasn't good enough, couldn't make him happy. She had no friends, she said, because he wouldn't let her have any, but deep down she knew it was due more to her own fears of closeness.

She was relieved when he finally left her. She had wanted the split but couldn't cut the cord herself. But after the relief came fear: "Now what do I do?"

Between the divorce settlement and her salary Lisa had enough money to return to school. This time she was determined to be a doctor and, much to her father's surprise, she was accepted into medical school. She was starting to feel good again, valued and respected. But then in medical school the self-doubts returned. Her supervisors said she was too slow, clumsy with simple procedures, disorganized. They criticized her for not ordering the right tests or getting lab results back in time. Only with the patients did she feel comfortable because with them she could be whomever she needed to be: kind and compassionate when that was needed; confrontive and demanding when that was called for.

Lisa also experienced a great deal of prejudice in medical school. She was older than most of the other students; she had a much different background; and she was a woman. Many of the patients called her "nurse" and some of the male patients didn't want "no lady doctor." She was hurt and angry because, like her parents, society and its institutions had also robbed her of her dignity.

THE DISINTEGRATING CULTURE

Psychological theories take on a different dimension when looked upon in light of the culture and time period from which they emanate. At the turn of the century, for instance, when Freud was formulating the system that would become the foundation of modern psychiatric thought, the cultural context was a formally structured, Victorian society. His theory that the primary origins of neuroses were the repression of unacceptable thoughts and feelings—aggressive and especially sexual—was entirely logical in this strict social context.

Now, nearly a century later, aggressive and sexual instincts are expressed more openly, and the social milieu is much more confused. What it means to be a man or a woman is much more ambiguous in modern western civilization than in turn-of-the-century Europe. Social, economic, and political structures are less fixed. The family unit and cultural roles are less defined and the very concept of "traditional" is unclear.

Though social factors may not be direct causes of BPD (or other forms of mental illness), they are, at the least, important indirect influences. Social factors interact with BPD in several ways and cannot be overlooked. First, if borderline pathology originates early in life—and much of the evidence points in this direction—an increase in the pathology is likely tied to the changing social patterns of family structure and parent-child interaction. In this regard, it is worthwhile to examine social changes in the area of childraising patterns, stability of home life, and child abuse and neglect.

Second, social changes of a more general nature have an exacerbative effect on people already suffering from the borderline syndrome. The lack of structure in American society, for example, is especially difficult for borderlines to handle, since they typically have immense problems creating structure for themselves. Women's shifting role patterns (career versus homemaker, for example) tend to aggravate identity problems. Indeed, some researchers attribute the prevalence of BPD among women to this social role conflict, now so widespread in our society. The increased severity of BPD in these cases may, in turn, be transmitted to future generations through parent-child interactions, multiplying the effects over time.

Third, the growing prominence of character disorders in general, and borderline personality more specifically, may be seen as a natural and inevitable response to—or an expression of—our contemporary culture. As Christopher Lasch notes in *The Culture of Narcissism:*

> Every society reproduces its culture—its norms, its underlying assumptions, its modes of organizing experience—in the individual, in the form of personality. As Durkheim said, personality is the individual socialized.[1]

For many, American culture has lost contact with the past and remains unconnected to the future. Our flooding of technical advancement and information requires greater individual commitment to solitary study and practice, thus sacrificing opportunities for socialization. Increasing divorce rates, expanding use of day care, and greater mobility have all contributed to a society that lacks constancy and reliability. Personal, intimate relationships become difficult or even impossible to achieve, and deep-seated loneliness, self-absorption, emptiness, anxiety, depression, and loss of self-esteem ensue.

The borderline syndrome represents a pathological response to these stresses. Without outside sources of stability and validation of worthiness, borderline symptoms of black-and-white thinking, self-destructiveness, extreme mood changes, impulsivity, poor relationships, impaired sense of identity, and anger become understandable reactions to our culture's tensions. Borderline traits, which may be present to some extent in most people, are being elicited—perhaps even bred—on a wide scale by the prevailing social conditions. *New York Times* writer Louis Sass put it this way:

> Each culture probably needs its own scapegoats as expressions of society's ills. Just as the hysterics of Freud's day exemplified the sexual repression of that era, the borderline, whose identity is split into many pieces, represents the fracturing of stable units in our society.[2]

Though the conventional wisdom is that borderline pathology has increased over the last few decades, some psychiatrists believe that the symptoms were just as common early in the twentieth century. They claim that the change is not in the prevalence of the disorder, but in the fact that it is now officially identified and defined, and so merely diagnosed more frequently. Even some of Freud's early cases, scrutinized in the light of current criteria, might be diagnosed today as borderline personalities.

This possibility, however, by no means diminishes the importance of the growing number of borderline patients who are ending up in psychiatrists' offices and of the growing recognition of borderline characteristics in the general population. In fact, the major reason why it has been identified and covered so widely in the clinical literature is its prevalence in both therapeutic settings and the general culture.

THE BREAKDOWN OF STRUCTURE: A FRAGMENTED SOCIETY

Few would dispute the proposition that society has become more fragmented since the end of World War II. Family structures in place for decades—the nuclear family, extended family, one wage-earner households, geographical stability—have been replaced by a wide assortment of patterns, movements, and trends. Divorce rates have soared. Drug and alcohol abuse and child abuse have skyrocketed. Crime, terrorism, and political assassination have become widespread, at times almost commonplace.

Some of these changes may be related to society's failure to achieve a kind of "social rapprochement." As noted in Chapter 3, during the separation-individuation phase, the infant ventures cautiously away from mother but returns to her reassuring warmth, familiarity, and acceptance. Disruption of this rapprochement cycle often results in a lack of trust, disturbed relationships, emptiness, anxiety, and an uncertain self-image—characteristics that make up the borderline syndrome. Similarly, it may be seen that contemporary culture interferes with a healthy "social rapprochement" by obstructing access to comforting anchors. In most areas of the country, the need for two incomes to maintain a decent standard of living forces many parents to relinquish parenting duties to others; precious few employers offer support in the way of paid parental leave or on-site day care for new parents. Jobs, as well as economic and social pressures, encourage frequent moves, and this geographical mobility, in turn, removes us from our stabilizing roots. We are losing (or have already lost) the comforts of neighborhood, nearby family, and consistent social roles.

When the accoutrements of custom disappear, they may be replaced by a sense of abandonment, of being adrift in unchartered waters. Our children lack a sense of history and belonging—of an anchored presence in the world. To establish a sense of control and comforting familiarity in an alienating society, the individual may resort to a wide range of pathological behavior—substance addiction, eating disorders, criminal behaviors, and so on.

Society's failure to provide rapprochement with reassuring, stabilizing bonds is reflected in the relentless series of sweeping societal movements over the past three decades. We have roller coastered from the explosive "We Decade" of the sixties, to the narcissistic "Me Decade" of the seventies, to the materialistic, fast-paced, "Whee Decade" of the eighties. Accompanying these external changes have been internal shifts in values: from the other-directed "peace, love, and brotherhood" of the sixties, to the "self-awareness" of the seventies, to the "self-seeking materialism" of the eighties.

One of the big losers in this shift to individualism and self-absorption has been group loyalties—devotion to family, neighborhood, church, occupation, and country. As society continues to foster detachment from people and institutions that provide reassuring rapprochement, individuals are responding in ways that virtually define the borderline syndrome: decreased sense of validated identity, worsening interpersonal relationships, isolation and loneliness, boredom, and (without the stabilizing force of group pressures) impulsivity.

Like the world of the borderline, ours in many ways is a world of massive contradictions. We presume to believe in peace, yet our streets, movies, television, and sports are filled with aggression and violence. We are a nation virtually founded on the principle of "Help thy neighbor," yet we have become one of the most politically conservative, self-absorbed, and materialistic societies in the history of humankind. Assertiveness and action are encouraged; reflection and introspection are equated with weakness and incompetency.

Contemporary social forces implore us to embrace a mythical polarity—black or white, right or wrong, good or bad—relying on our nostalgia for simpler times, for our own childhoods. The political system presents candidates who adopt polar stances: "I'm right, the other guy is wrong;" America is good; the Soviet Union is "the Evil Empire." Religious factions exhort us to believe that theirs' is the only route to salvation. The legal system, built on the premise that one is either guilty or not guilty with little or no room for gray areas, perpetuates the myth that life is intrinsically fair and justice can be attained—that is, when something bad does happen, it is necessarily someone's fault and that person should pay.

The flood of information and leisure alternatives in our increasingly affluent and highly technical society makes it difficult to establish priorities in living. Ideally, we—as individuals and as a society—attempt to achieve a balance between nurturing the body and the mind, between work and leisure, between altruism and self-interest. But in an increasingly materialistic society it is a small step from assertiveness to aggressiveness, from individualism to alienation, from self-preservation to self-absorption.

The ever-growing reverence for science and technology has led to an obsessive pursuit of precision. Calculators and computers replace memorized multiplication tables and slide rules. Velcro deprives children of learning how to tie shoelaces. Creativity and intellectual diligence are sacrificed to convenience and precision.

All these attempts to impose order and fairness on a naturally random and unfair universe endorse the borderline's futile struggle to choose only black or white, right or wrong, good or bad. But the world is neither intrinsically fair nor exact; it is composed of subtleties that require less simplistic approaches. A healthy civilization can accept the uncomfortable ambiguities. Attempts to eradicate or ignore uncertainty tend only to encourage a borderline society.

We would be naive to believe that the cumulative effect of all this change—the excruciating pull of opposing forces—has had no effect on our psyches. In a sense, we all live in a kind of "borderland"—between the prosperous, healthy, high-technology America on the one hand, and the underbelly of poverty, homelessness, drug abuse, and mental illness on the other; between the dream of a sane, safe, secure world and the insane nightmare of nuclear holocaust.

The price tag of social change has come in the form of stress and stress-related physical disorders, such as heart attacks, strokes, and hypertension. We must now confront the possibility that mental illness has become part of the psychological price.

DREAD OF THE FUTURE

Over the past two decades, therapeutic settings have seen a basic change in psychopathology from symptom neuroses to character disorders. As far back as 1975, psychiatrist Peter L. Giovachinni wrote, "Clinicians are constantly faced with the seemingly increasing number of patients who do not fit current diagnostic categories. [They suffer not from] definitive symptoms but from vague ill-defined complaints . . . When I refer to this type of patient, practically everyone knows to whom I am referring."[3]

In the eighties, of course, such reports have become commonplace, as personality disorders have replaced classical neurosis as the prominent pathology. Which social and cultural factors have influenced this change in pathology? Many social observers, including Lasch, believe that one factor is our devaluation of the past:

> To live for the moment is the prevailing passion—to live for yourself, not for your predecessors or posterity. We are fast losing the sense of historical continuity, the sense of belonging to a succession of generations originating in the past and stretching into the future.[4]

This loss of historical continuity works both ways in terms of time. Devaluation of the past breaks the perceptual link to the future, which becomes a vast unknown, a source of dread as much as hope. Time is perceived as isolated points instead of as a logical, continuous string of events influenced by past achievement and present action.

The threat of nuclear annihilation is one contributor to our lack of faith in the past and our dread of the future. Empirical studies with adolescents and children consistently show "awareness of the danger, hopelessness about surviving, a shortened time perspective, and pessimism about being able to reach life goals. Suicide is mentioned again and again as a strategy for dealing with the threat."[5] Other studies have found that the threat of nuclear war rushes children to a kind of "early adulthood," similar to the type witnessed in those preborderline children who are forced to take control of families that are out of control due to BPD, alcoholism, and other mental disorders.[6] According to Berkeley child psychologist Edward Levin, a common response from adolescents when asked, "What do you picture yourself doing ten years from now?" is, "We'll all be dead."[7]

The borderline, as we have seen, personifies this orientation to the "now." With little interest in the past, the borderline is almost a cultural amnesiac; his cupboard of warm memories (which sustain most of us in troubled times) is bare. As a result, he is doomed to suffer torment with no breathers, no concrete memories of happier times to get him through the tough periods. Unable to learn from his mistakes, he is doomed to repeat them.

Parents who fear the future are not likely to be engrossed by the needs of the next generation. A modern parent, emotionally detached and alienated—yet at the same time pampering and overindulgent—becomes a likely candidate to mold future borderline personalities.

THE JUNGLE OF INTERPERSONAL RELATIONSHIPS

Perhaps the hallmark changes over the last two decades have come in the area of sexual mores, roles, and practices—from the suppressed sexuality of the fifties to the "free-love" and "open marriage" ethics of the sixties' sexual revolution to the massive sexual reevaluation in the eighties, resulting in large part from the fear of AIDS.

Societal forces have been making deep and lasting friendships, love affairs, and marriages increasingly difficult to achieve and maintain. Half of the couples who married in the seventies will divorce in the eighties.[8] Lasch has noted that, "As social life becomes more and more warlike and barbaric, personal relations, which ostensibly provide relief from those conditions, take on the character of combat."[9]

Borderlines may be well suited for this kind of combat. The narcissistic man's need to dominate and be idolized fits well with the borderline woman's ambivalent need to be controlled and punished. Borderline women often marry at a young age to escape the chaos of family life. They cling to dominating husbands with whom they recreate the miasma of home life. Both may enter a kind of "Slap! . . . 'Thanks, I needed that'" sadomasochistic dyad. Less typical, but still common, is a reversal of these roles, with a borderline male linked with a narcissistic female partner.

Masochism is a prominent characteristic of borderline relationships. Dependency coupled with pain elicits the familiar refrain "love hurts." As a child, the borderline experiences pain and confusion in trying to establish a maturing relationship with his mother or primary caregiver. Later in life, other partners—spouse, friends, minister, doctor—renew this early confusion. Criticism or abuse particularly reinforces the borderline's self-image of worthlessness. Lisa's later relationships with her husband and supervisors, for example, recapitulated the profound feelings of worthlessness that were ingrained by the constant criticisms of her father.

Sometimes the borderline's masochistic suffering transforms into sadism. For example, Ann would sometimes encourage her husband Larry to drink, knowing about his drinking problem. Then she'd instigate a fight, fully aware of Larry's violent propensities when drunk. Following a beating, Ann would wear her bruises like battle scars, reminding Larry of his violence, and insisting they go out in public, where Ann would explain away her marks as such "accidents" as "running into doors."

After each episode, Larry would feel profoundly regretful and humiliated, while Ann would present herself as a long-suffering martyr. In this way Ann used her beatings to exact punishment from Larry. The question of the real victim in this relationship became increasingly vague.

Even when a relationship is apparently ruptured, the borderline comes crawling back for more punishment, feeling he deserves the denigration. The punishment is comfortably familiar, easier to cope with than the frightening prospect of change and solitude.

A typical scenario for modern social relationships is the "overlapping lover" pattern—the need to establish a new romance before severing a current one. The borderline exemplifies this constant need for partnership: As the borderline climbs the jungle gym of relationships, he cannot let go of the last bar until he has firmly grasped the next. Typically, the borderline will not leave his current, abusive spouse until a new "white knight" is at least visible on the horizon.

Periods of relaxed social-sexual mores and less structured romantic relationships (such as in the late-sixties and seventies) are more difficult for borderlines to handle; increased freedom and lack of structure paradoxically imprison the borderline, who is greatly handicapped in devising his own individual system of values. Conversely, the sexual withdrawal period of the late-eighties (due in part to the AIDS epidemic) can be ironically helpful for borderline personalities. Social fears enforce strict boundaries that can be crossed only at the risk of great physical harm; impulsivity and promiscuity now have severe penalties. This external structure can help protect the borderline from his self-destructiveness.

SHIFTING GENDER ROLE PATTERNS

Earlier in the century, social roles were fewer, well-defined and much more easily combined. Mother was domestic, working in the home, in charge of the children. Outside interests, such as school involvement, hobbies, and charity work, flowed naturally from these duties. Father's work and community visibility also combined smoothly. And, together, their roles worked harmoniously for the most part.

The complexities of modern society, however, dictate that the individual develop a plethora of social roles—many of which do not come together so easily. The working mother, for example, has two distinct roles and must struggle to perform both well. The policies of most employers demand that the working mom keep the home and workplace separate; as a result, many mothers feel guilty or embarrassed when problems from one impact the other.

A working father also finds work and home roles compartmentalized. He is no longer the owner of the local grocery who lives above the store. More likely, he works miles from home and has much less time to be with his family. Furthermore, the modern dad plays an increasingly participatory role with familial responsibility.

Shifting role patterns over the last twenty-five years are central to theories on why BPD is so prevalent among women. The latest studies report that approximately two-thirds of people afflicted with BPD are women (see Chapter 1). In the past, a woman had essentially one life course—getting married (usually in her late teens or early twenties), having children, staying in the home to raise those children, and repressing any career ambitions. Today, in contrast, a young woman is faced with a bewildering array of role models and expectations—from the single career woman, to the married career woman, to the traditional nurturing mother, to the "supermom," who strives to combine marriage, career, and children successfully.

Men have also experienced new roles and expectations, of course, but not nearly so wide-ranging—nor conflicting—as women. Today, men are expected to be more sensitive and open and to take a larger part in childraising than in previous eras, yet these qualities and responsibilities usually fit within the overall role of "provider" or "coprovider." It is the rare man who, for example, abandons, or even seriously considers abandoning, career ambitions for the role of "househusband"—nor is this expected of him.

Men have fewer adjustments to make during the evolution of relationships and marriages. For example, relocations are usually dictated by the man's career needs, since he is most often the primary wage earner. Throughout pregnancy, birth, and child rearing, few changes occur in the man's day-to-day reality. The woman not only endures the physical demands of pregnancy and childbirth and must leave her job to give birth, but it is also she who must make the transition back to work or give up her career. And yet in many dual-earner households, although it may not be openly stated, the woman simply assumes the primary responsibility for the maintenance of the home. She is the one who usually adjusts her plans to stay home with a sick child or waits for the repairman to come.

Though women have struggled successfully to achieve increased social and career options, they may have had to pay an exacting price in the process: excruciating life decisions about career, families, and children; strains on their relationships with their children and husband; the stress resulting from making and living with these decisions; and confusion about who they are and who they want to be. From this perspective, it is understandable that women should be more vulnerable to BPD, a disorder in which identity and role confusion are such central components.

Yet despite the statistical evidence pointing to BPD as a "woman's illness," some clinicians claim that there are not more women borderlines today; rather, their symptoms are just more evident. The borderline symptom of angry outbursts, for example, socially unacceptable for women in previous eras, is now allowed to surface. For today's woman, living in an era that accepts—even encourages—open and honest expression of emotion and communication, releasing anger and other deep emotions has come to be recognized as a healthy antidote to repression. Career women particularly are expected to be assertive in their jobs and many "assertiveness training" seminars are directed at working women. Suddenly, after centuries of trying to mold "shy, demure creatures," and many girls are still brought up this way, our male-dominated society encourages women to express aggressive behavior and deep emotion—and simultaneously expects them to shut it off at will.

To illustrate another type of cultural bias, one study found that BPD is diagnosed with almost equal frequency among both Hispanic men and women, as opposed to most studies, which find a higher prevalence of borderline women than borderline men. The researchers speculate that the reason may be a combination of sociocultural differences and a kind of clinician bias:

> It is possible that borderline personality disorder was overdiagnosed among the Hispanic men in our study because most of the clinicians were white and did not speak Spanish... Behavior within the normal limits of the Puerto Rican culture may be regarded as deviant when judged outside its original social context; for example, the display of exuberant mannerisms and dramatic behavior by a Hispanic man may lead a clinician unfamiliar with such demeanor to perceive impulsivity, inappropriate anger, and affective instability, all of which are DSM-III criteria for borderline personality disorder.[10]

Similarly, predominantly white and English-speaking therapists may dismiss traits, such as histrionic behavior, poor control of anger and impulsiveness, as mannerisms typical of the Hispanic woman—or, more closely, the *stereotype* of the Hispanic woman—when they should be more objective in evaluating these as symptoms.

Whether BPD is a "woman's illness" is a controversial issue, and the argument cannot be settled here. Suffice it to say that, just as the price for women's increased freedom may be the jarring turmoil of role confusion, the price of increased responsibility may be a whole set of undesirable (and traditionally male) behaviors. The combination of all these forces can at least exacerbate the severity of borderline personality among women.

Sexual Orientation and Borderlines

Sexual orientation is also a part of the borderline's role confusion. In line with this theory, some researchers estimate a significantly increased rate of homosexuality, bisexuality and sexual perversions among borderlines.[11,12] Homosexuality in the borderline may originate early in childhood, resulting from a number of possible factors: lack of role models, sexual assaults, an insatiable need for affection and attention, discomfort with one's own body, and inconsistent sexual information.

FAMILY AND CHILD REARING PATTERNS

Since the end of World War II, our society has experienced striking changes in family and child-rearing patterns:

- The institution of the nuclear family has been in steady decline. Largely due to divorce, it is estimated that 58 percent of American children spend a significant part of their lives in a single-parent home.[13]
- Alternative family structures (such as "blended families," in which a single parent with children combines with another one-parent household to form a new family unit) have led to situations in which many children are raised by persons other than their birth parents.
- Due to increased geographical mobility, the traditional extended family, with grandparents, siblings, cousins, and other family relations living in close proximity, is almost extinct, leaving the nuclear family virtually unsupported.
- The number of women working outside the home has increased dramatically. In 1980, more than half the mothers in the U.S. were employed outside the home, and current estimates indicate that by 1990, 75 percent of all American mothers will work. Ten times as many mothers of preschool-age children work now as did in 1945.[14]
- As a result of women working outside the home, more children than ever before are being placed in various forms of day care—and at a much earlier age. The number of infants in day care has increased 45 percent since 1980.[15]
- The evidence clearly suggests that the incidence of child physical and sexual abuse has increased significantly over the past decade.[16]

What are the psychological effects of these child-rearing changes—on both children and parents? Though many of these changes (such as blended families) are too new to be the subject of intensive studies, psychiatrists and developmental experts generally agree that children growing up in settings marked by turmoil, instability, or abuse are at much greater risk for emotional and mental problems in adolescence and adulthood. Moreover, parents in such environments are much more likely to develop stress, guilt, depression, lower self-esteem—all characteristics associated with BPD.

James Masterson notes that governments with extensive social welfare systems—such as the Scandinavian countries and increasingly the United States—promote a social dependency that discourages autonomy and increases borderline and sociopathic behaviors among the citizenry. In Israel the primary mode of child rearing is often the kibbutz nursery, where the central caregivers are not the birth parents but rather a collection of parental figures. This type of family structure may develop soldiers and other cogs in a cooperative society but tends to diffuse the task of separation and individuation and to mute the growth of an autonomous self and a sense of individuality. In Japan the mother characteristically initially indulges the grandiosity of the child and later controls him through use of guilt. Masterson feels that this results in a nation prominent in smooth social functioning but severely lacking in personal qualities of creativity, autonomy, and intimacy.[17]

Infant Day Care: The Unknown Quantity

During the first months of life, the infant begins developing emotional and cognitive awareness of self and the nurturing "other" (see Chapter 3). The baby is learning about herself, developing an ego base. Simultaneously, the parents are also learning about themselves as nurturers. A two-way communication-feedback system develops—the baby's first exposure to social communication. The infant experiences emotion and at the same time learns to elicit and respond to the emotions of nurturant adults.[18]

According to T. Berry Brazelton and other noted developmental experts, these early months are a crucial precursor for future emotional development, response patterns, and self-esteem: "The experience of completing an anticipated act of social communication closes a feedback cycle, creating a sense of mastery that confirms children's sense of self and fuels them toward further development."[19]

The weight of the evidence suggests that an infant who is deprived of this chance to learn about herself will be more likely to experience impaired emotional and cognitive development. Later in life, the child is much more likely to have problems with identity, self-esteem, security, separations, and social relationships—all issues, as we have seen, in the borderline syndrome.

The effects of day care on parents are also significant. Study after study has shown day care to be a primary source of stress for working parents.[20] Parents deprived of the chance to stay at home during their baby's early months are more apt to feel depressed, cheated, guilty, and inadequate as parents. Mothers particularly are susceptible to feelings of powerlessness and guilt and frequently form defenses to cope with the feelings: (1) denial that the feelings are real; (2) projecting the role of "good mother" onto the day-care provider and adopting the role of "bad mother" herself, or vice-versa; and (3) detaching emotionally from the child because of the pain of separation.[21]

Some recent studies on infant day care indicate that extensive day care initiated in the first year of life may lead to insecure mother-infant attachments and noncompliance, aggression, and insecurity later in childhood.[22] The conclusions of these studies are disputed by some mental health professionals who point out the positive aspects of day care for both the cognitive and social development of the child. Because the phenomenon of infant day care is simply so new, the long-term consequences may not be fully understood for many years. "Almost an entire generation of children is being raised in a way that has never been done before," writes noted child expert and Yale psychologist Edward Zigler. "We won't know the ultimate effects until these infants have grown into adults."[23]

Child Abuse and Neglect: Destroyer of Trust

Child abuse and neglect are becoming increasingly recognizable health problems. Even conservative estimates report that one million children per year in the United States are mistreated by parents. More than 200,000 children per year are sexually abused and 200,000 to 300,000 are psychologically abused.[24] Some studies estimate that 25 percent of girls experience some form of sexual abuse (from parents or others) by the time they reach adulthood.[25]

Characteristics of physically abused preschool-age children include: inhibition, depression, attachment difficulties, behavior problems (such as hyperactivity and severe tantrums), poor impulse control, aggressiveness, and peer-relation problems.[26]

"Violence begets violence," said John Lennon, and this is

particularly true in the case of battered children. Because those who are abused often become abusers themselves, this problem can self-perpetuate over many decades and generations.

The incidence of abuse or neglect among borderlines is high enough to be a factor that separates BPD from other personality disorders. Verbal or psychological abuse is the most common form, followed by physical and then sexual abuse. Physical and sexual abuse may be more dramatic in nature, but the emotionally abused child can suffer total loss of self-esteem.

Emotional child abuse can take several forms:

- **Degradation**—constantly devaluing the child's achievements and magnifying misbehavior. After awhile, the child becomes convinced that he really is bad or worthless.
- **Unavailability**—psychologically absent parents show little interest in the child's development, and provide no affection in times of need.
- **Domination**—use of extreme threats to control the child's behavior. Some child development experts have compared this form of abuse to the techniques used by terrorists to brainwash captives.[27]

The pattern of the neglected child, as described by psychologist Hugh Missildine, mirrors the dilemmas of borderlines in later life:

> If you suffered from neglect in childhood, it may cause you to go from one person to another, hoping that someone will supply whatever is missing. You may not be able to care much about yourself, and think marriage will end this, and then find yourself in the alarming situation of being married but emotionally unattached . . . Moreover, the person who [has] neglect in his background is always restless and anxious because he cannot obtain emotional satisfaction . . . These restless, impulsive moves help to create the illusion of living emotionally . . . Such a person may, for example, be engaged to be married to one person and simultaneously be maintaining sexual relationships with two or three others. Anyone who offers admiration and respect has appeal to them—and because their need for affection is so great, their ability to discriminate is severely impaired.[28]

From what we understand of the roots of BPD (see Chapter 3), abuse, neglect, or prolonged separations early in childhood can greatly disrupt the developing infant's establishment of trust. Self-esteem and autonomy are crippled. The abilities to cope with separation and to form identity do not proceed normally. As they become adults, abused children may recapitulate frustrating relationships with others. Pain and punishment may become associated with closeness—they come to believe that "love hurts." As the borderline matures, self-mutilation may become the proxy for the abusive parent.

Children of Divorce: The Disappearing Father

Due primarily to divorce, more children than ever before are being raised without the physical and/or emotional presence of their father. Because most courts award children to the mother in custody cases, the large majority of single-parent homes are headed by mothers. Even in cases of joint custody or liberal visitation rights, the father, who is likely to remarry sooner after divorce and start a new family, often fades from the child's upbringing.

The recent trend in child raising, toward a more equal sharing of parental responsibilities between mother and father, makes divorce even more upsetting for the child. Children clearly benefit from dual parenting, but they also lose more when the marriage dissolves, especially if the breakup occurs during the formative years when the child still has many crucial developmental stages to hurdle.

Studies on the effects of divorce typically report profound upset, neediness, regression, and acute separation anxiety related to fears of abandonment in children of preschool age.[29] A significant number are found to be depressed[30] or antisocial in later stages of childhood.[31]

During separation and divorce, the child's need for physical intimacy increases. For example, it is typical for a child at the time of separation to ask a parent to sleep with him. If the practice continues, becoming the parent's need as well, the child's own sense of autonomy and bodily integrity may be threatened. This, combined with the loneliness and severe narcissistic injury caused by the divorce places some children at high risk for developmental arrest or, if the need for affection and reassurance becomes desperate, for sexual abuse. A father separated from the home may demand more time with the child in order to relieve his own feelings of loneliness and deprivation. If the child becomes a lightening rod for his father's resentment and bitterness, he may again be at higher risk for abuse.

In many situations of parental separation, the child becomes the pawn in a destructive battle between his parents. One father, who usually ignored his visitation privileges, suddenly demanded that his daughter stay with him whenever he was angry at her mother. These visits were usually unpleasant for the child as well as for her father and his new family, yet were used as punishment for his ex-wife, who would feel guilty and powerless at his demands. Another child became embroiled in conflicts between his divorced parents when his mother periodically took his father back to court to extract more child support monies. Bribes of material gifts or threats to cut off support for school or home maintenance are common weapons used between continuously skirmishing parents; the bribes and threats are usually more harmful to the children than they are to the parents.

Children may even be drawn into court battles and forced to testify about their parents. In these situations neither the parents, nor the courts, nor social welfare organizations can protect the child, who is often left with a sense of overwhelming helplessness (conflicts continue despite his input), or of intoxicating power (his testimony controls the battle between his parents). He may feel enraged at his predicament and yet fearful that he could be abandoned by everyone. All of this becomes fertile ground for the development of borderline pathology.

In addition to divorce, the past two decades have witnessed the maturing of children of thousands of World War II, Korean War, and Viet Nam War veterans and of many prison-camp and concentration-camp survivors. Not only were many of these fathers absent during significant portions of their children's development, but many were found to develop post-traumatic stress disorders and delayed mourning ("impacted grief") related to combat that also influenced child development.[32] By 1970, 40 percent of World War II and Korean War POWs had met violent death by suicide, homicide, or auto-accident (mostly one-car single-occupant accidents).[33] Children of holocaust survivors often have severe emotional difficulties, rooted in their parents' massive psychic trauma.[34]

The "absent father syndrome" can lead to pathological consequences. Often in families torn by divorce or death, the mother tries to compensate by becoming the ideal parent, arranging every aspect of her child's life; naturally, the child has limited opportunity to develop his own identity. Without the buffering of another parent, the mother-child link can be too close to allow for healthy separating.

Though the mother often seeks to replace the missing father, in many cases it is actually the child who tries to replace the absent father. In the absence of father, the symbiotic intensity of the bond with mother is greatly magnified. The child grows up with an idealized view of the mother and fantasies of forever trying to please her. And a parent's dependence on the child may persist, interfering with growth and individuation, planting the seeds of BPD.

Permissive Child-Rearing Practices

Modern permissive child-rearing practices, involving the transfer of traditional parental functions to outside agencies— the school, mass media, industry—have significantly altered the quality of parent-child relationships. Parental "instinct" has been supplanted by a reliance on books and child-rearing experts. Child rearing, in many households, takes a back seat to the demands of dual careers. "Quality time" becomes a guilt-induced euphemism for "not enough time."

Many parents overcompensate by lavishing attention on the child's practical and recreational needs, yet providing little real warmth. Narcissistic parents perceive their children as extensions of themselves or as objects/possessions, rather than as separate human beings. As a result, the child suffocates in emotionally distant attention, leading to an exaggerated sense of his own importance, regressive defenses, and loss of a sense of self.

Geographical Mobility: Where Is Home?

We are moving more than ever before. Greater geographical mobility can bring rich educational benefits and cultural exchange for a child, but numerous relocations are often also accompanied by a feeling of rootlessness. Some investigators have found that children who move frequently and stay in one place for only short periods of time often have confused responses, or no response at all, to the simple question, "Where is your home?"[35]

Because hypermobility is typically correlated with career-oriented lifestyles and job demands, one or both parents in mobile families tend to work long hours and so are less available to their children. Having few enough constants in their environment to provide ballast for development, mobility adds another disruptive force—the world turns into a menagerie of changing places and faces. Such children may grow up bored and lonely, looking for constant stimulation. Continually forced to adapt to new situations and people, they may lose the stable sense of self encouraged by firm community anchors. Though socially graceful, they typically feel they are gracefully faking it.

With increasing geographical mobility, the stability of the neighborhood, community school systems, church and civic institutions, and friendships are weakened. Generations are becoming separated by long distances, and the extended family is lost for emotional support and child care. Children are raised without knowing their grandparents, aunts, uncles, and cousins, losing a strong connection to the past and a source of love and warmth to nurture healthy emotional growth.

5

Understanding and Healing

"Now *here,* you see, it takes all the running *you* can do to keep in the same place. If you want to get somewhere else, you must run at least twice as fast as that."
—*Lewis Carroll*, Through the Looking Glass

"I FEEL LIKE I have a void in me that I can never quite fill." Elizabeth, an attractive, witty twenty-eight-year-old woman, was originally referred for therapy by her family doctor. She had been married for six years to a man who was ten years older than she and had been her boss at one time. Five months before, she had given birth to her first child, a daughter, and was now severely depressed.

She yearned for something she could call her own, something that would show "the rest of the world knew I was here." Inside, she felt her "real self" was a swamp of childish emotions, and that she was always hiding her feelings, which were "ugly and bad." These realizations turned into self-hate; she wanted to give up.

By her count, Elizabeth had had nine extramarital affairs over the previous six years—all with men she met through work.

They began soon after the death of her father. Most were relationships that she totally controlled, first by initiating them and later by ending them. She had found it exciting that these men seemed so puzzled by her advances and then by her sudden rejections. She enjoyed the physical closeness, but acknowledged she dreaded being too emotionally involved. Although she controlled these relationships, she never found them sexually satisfying; nor was she sexually responsive to her husband. She said she felt safer using sex to "equalize" relationships, to stay in control. Her intellect and personality, she felt, were not enough to hold a man.

Reared in a working-class Catholic family, Elizabeth had three older brothers and a younger sister, who had drowned in a swimming accident at age five. Elizabeth was only eight at the time and had little understanding of the event except to observe her mother becoming more withdrawn.

For as long as Elizabeth could remember, her mother had been hypercritical, constantly accusing Elizabeth of being "bad." When she was a young girl, her mother insisted that she attend church with her, and forced her father to construct an altar in Elizabeth's bedroom. Elizabeth felt closer to her father, a passive and quiet man, who was dominated by his wife. As she entered puberty, he became more distant and less affectionate.

Growing up, Elizabeth was quiet and shy. Her mother disapproved of her involvement with boys and closely watched her friendships with girls; she was expected to have "acceptable" friends. Her brothers were always favored; she would kid with them, trying to be "one of the guys." Elizabeth achieved good grades in high school but was discouraged from going to college. After graduation, she began working full time as a secretary.

As time went on, the conflicts with her mother escalated. Even in high school, Elizabeth's mother had denounced her as a "tramp" and constantly accused her of promiscuity, although she had had no sexual experience. After a while, having endured the shouting contests with her mother, she saved enough money to move out on her own.

During this turmoil, Elizabeth's boss separated from his wife, and was in the midst of a painful divorce. Elizabeth offered solace and sympathy. He reciprocated with encouragement and support. They began dating, and married soon after his divorce was finalized. Naturally, her mother berated her for marrying a divorced man, particularly one who was ten years older and a lapsed Catholic.

Her father remained detached. One year after Elizabeth married, he died.

Five years later, her marriage was disintegrating, and Elizabeth was blaming her husband. She saw him as a "thief" who had stolen her youth. She was only nineteen when she met him, and needed to be taken care of so badly that she traded in her youth for security—the years when she could have been "experimenting with what I wanted to be, could be, should have been."

In the early stages of treatment, Elizabeth began to talk of her most recent and most important affair: David was twelve years older, a longtime family friend, and the parish priest. He was someone known and loved by her whole family, especially by her mother. He was the only man to whom Elizabeth felt attached. This was the only relationship that she did not control. On and off, over a period of two years, he would abruptly terminate the affair and then restore it. Later, she confessed to her psychiatrist that David was the father of her child. Her husband was apparently unaware.

Elizabeth became more withdrawn. Her relationship with her husband, who was frequently away traveling, deteriorated. She became more alienated from her mother and brothers and allowed her few friendships to flounder. She resisted attempts to include her husband in therapy, feeling he and her doctor colluded and favored "his side." So, even therapy reinforced her belief that she couldn't trust or place faith in anyone because she would only be disappointed. All her thoughts and feelings seemed to be laden with contradictions, as if she were in a maze of dead end paths. Her sexuality seemed the only way out of the maze.

Her therapist was often the target of her complaints because he was the one "in control." She would yell at him, accuse him of being incompetent, threaten to stop therapy. She hoped he would get mad, yell back, and stop seeing her, or become defensive and plead with her to stay. But he did neither, and she railed against his unflappability as evidence that he had no feelings.

Even though she was accustomed to her husband's frequent business trips, she started to become more frightened when left alone. During these trips, for reasons not yet clear to her, she slept on the floor. When he returned, she raged constantly at him. She became more depressed. Suicide became less an option than a destiny, as if everything were leading to that end.

Elizabeth's vision of reality became more frail: She yearned to be psychotic, to live in a fantasy world where she could "go anywhere" in her mind. The world would be so far removed from reality, no one—not even the best psychiatrist—could get to her and "see what's underneath."

In her daydreams she envisioned herself protected by a powerful, handsome man who actively appreciated all of her admirable qualities and was endlessly attentive. She fantasized him to be a previous teacher, her doctor, the family veterinarian, and, eventually her psychiatrist. Although all of these men were perceived as powerful, they were also recognized as unavailable. But in her fantasies they were overwhelmed by her charm and drawn irresistibly to her. When reality did not follow her script—when an attractive man did not aggressively flirt with her—she became despondent and self-loathing, feeling she was not attractive enough.

Everywhere she looked she saw women who were prettier, smarter, better. She wished her hair was prettier, her eyes a different color, her skin clearer. When she looked in a mirror, she saw distortions—not a beautiful young woman, but an old hag with sagging breasts, a wide waist, plump calves. She despised herself for being a woman, whose only value was her beauty. She longed to be a man, "so my mind would count."

In her second year of outpatient therapy, Elizabeth experienced several losses, including the death of a favorite uncle to whom she had grown close. She was haunted by recurring dreams and nightmares that she could not remember when she awoke. She became more depressed and suicidal and was finally hospitalized.

With the aid of hypnosis she began recalling traumatic childhood events, opening up a Pandora's box of flooding memories. She recalled severe physical beatings by her mother and then began to remember her mother's sexual abuses—episodes in which her mother had inflicted vaginal douches and enemas and fondled her in order to "clean" her vagina. These rituals began when Elizabeth was about eight, shortly after her sister's death, and persisted until puberty. She recalled looking into her mother's face and noting a benign, peaceful expression; these were the only times Elizabeth could remember when it appeared her mother was not disapproving.

Elizabeth recalled sitting alone in the closet for many hours and often sleeping on the floor for fear of being molested in her bed. Sometimes she would sleep with a ribbon or award she had won in school. She found these actions to be comforting and continued them as an adult, often favoring the floor for the bed and spending time alone in a quiet room or dark closet.

In the hospital Elizabeth spoke of the different sides to her personality. She described fantasies of being different people and even gave these personality fragments separate names. These persona were independent women, had unique talents, and were either admired by others or snobbishly avoided social contacts. Elizabeth felt that whenever she accomplished something or was successful, it was due to the talents of one of these separate personality **segments. She had** great difficulty integrating these components into a stable self-concept.

Nonetheless, she did recognize these as personality fragments and they never took over her functioning. She suffered no clear periods of amnesia or dissociation, nor were her symptoms considered aspects of multiple personality disorder—although this syndrome is frequently associated with BPD.

Elizabeth used these "other women" to express the desires and feelings that she herself was forced to repress. Believing she was worthless, she felt these other partial identities were separate, stronger entities. Gradually, in the hospital, she learned that this simply was not so, that they were always a part of her. Recognizing this gave her relief and hope. She began to believe that Elizabeth was stronger and less crazy than she had imagined and this marked a turning point in her life.

But she could not claim victory yet. Like a field officer, she marshaled the separate sides of her personality to stand before her and found that they could not go into battle without a unifying resolve. Elizabeth—the core of her being—was still afraid of change, love, and success, still searched in vain for safety, still fled from relationships. Coming to accept herself was going to be more difficult than she had ever imagined.

After six weeks Elizabeth left the hospital and continued in outpatient care. As she improved, her relationship with her husband deteriorated. But instead of blaming herself, as she typically did, she attempted to resolve the differences and to stay with him. She distanced herself from unhealthy contacts with family members. She developed more positive self-esteem. She began taking college courses and did remarkably well, achieving academic awards. She slept with her first award under her pillow, as she did when she was a child. Later she entered law school and received merit awards for being the top student in her class. She developed new relationships, with men and women, and found she was comfortable in these, without having to be in control. She became more content with her own femaleness.

Little by little, Elizabeth started to heal. She felt "the curtains raising." She compared the feeling to looking for a valuable antique in a dark attic filled with junk—she knew that it was in there somewhere but couldn't see it because of all the clutter. When she finally did spot it, she couldn't get to it because it was "buried under a pile of useless garbage." But now and then she could see a clear path to the object, as if a flash of lightning had illuminated the room for a brief instant.

The flashes were all too brief. Old doubts reared up like ugly faces in an amusement-park fun house. Many times she felt as if she were going up a down escalator, struggling up one step only to fall down two. She kept wanting to sell herself short and give credit to others for her accomplishments. But her first real challenge—becoming an attorney—was almost a reality. Five years before, she wouldn't have been able to talk about school, much less have had the courage to enroll. The timbre of her depressions began to change: Her depression over failing was now evolving, she recognized, into a fear of success.

GROWING AND CHANGING

"Change is real hard work!" Elizabeth often noted. It requires conscious retreat from unhealthy situations and the will to build healthier foundations. It entails coping with drastic interruption of a long-established equilibrium.

Like Darwinian evolution, individual change happens almost imperceptibly, with much trial and error. The individual instinctively resists mutation. He may live in a kind of swamp, but it is *his* swamp; he knows where everything is, what's in all the bogs and marshes. To leave his swamp means venturing into the unknown and perhaps falling into an even worse swamp.

For the borderline, whose world is so clearly demarcated by black and white parameters, the uncertainty of change is even more threatening. She may clutch at one extreme for fear of falling uncontrollably into the abyss of another. The borderline anorexic, for example, starves herself out of the terror that eating—even a tiny morsel—will lead to total loss of control and irrevocable obesity.

The borderline's fear of change involves a basic distrust of her "brakes." In healthier people these psychic brakes allow a gradual descent from the pinnacle of a mood or behavior to a gentle stop in the "gray zone" of the incline. Afraid that his set of brakes won't hold, the borderline believes that he won't be able to stop, that he will slide out of control to the bottom of the hill.

Change, however gradual, requires the alteration of automatic reflexes. The borderline is in a situation much like a child playing a game of "Make me blink" or "Make me laugh," struggling valiantly to stifle a blink or a laugh while another child waves her hand or makes funny faces. Such reflexes, established over many years, can be adjusted only with conscious, motivated effort.

Adults sometimes engage in similar contests of will. A man who encounters an angry barking dog in a strange neighborhood resists the automatic reflex to run away from the danger. He recognizes that if he runs, the dog would likely catch up with him and present an even greater threat. Instead, he does the opposite—he stands perfectly still, allows the dog to sniff him, and then walks slowly on.

Psychological change requires resisting unproductive automatic reflexes and consciously and willfully choosing other alternatives—choices that are different, even opposite, from the automatic reflex—sometimes these new ways of behaving are frightening, but they hopefully are more efficient ways of coping.

The Beginnings of Change: Self-Assessment

Change for the borderline involves more of a fine-tuning than a total reconstruction. It is best initiated gradually, with only slight alterations at first, and must begin with self-assessment: One must first recognize his current position and understand in which direction modification must progress.

Imagine personality as a series of intersecting lines, each representing a specific character trait (see figure 5-1). The extremes of each trait are located at the ends of the line, with the middle ground in the center. For example, on the "conscientiousness at work" line, one end might symbolize obsessive over concern or "workaholicism" and the other end "irresponsibility"; the middle would be an attitude somewhere between these two extremes, such as "calm professionalism." On the "concern about appearance" line, one end might exemplify "narcissistic attention to surface looks," and the other end, "total disinterest." Ideally, one's personality make-up would look like the spokes of a perfectly round wheel, with all these lines intersecting near their midpoints in the wheel "hub."

Of course, no one is completely centered all the time. It is important to identify each line in which change is desired and locate one's position on that line in relation to the middle. Change then becomes a process of knowing where you are and how far you want to go towards the middle. Except at the extreme ends, no particular locus is intrinsically "better" or "worse" than another. It is a matter of knowing oneself (locating oneself on the line) and moving in the adaptive direction.

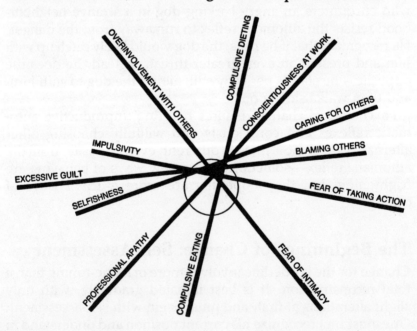

Figure 5-1: Personality as a series of intersecting lines

For example, if we isolate the "caring for others" line (see figure 5-2), one end ("self-sacrificing over concern") represents the point where concern for others interferes with taking care of oneself; such a person may need to dedicate himself totally to others in order to feel worthwhile. This position may be perceived as a kind of "selfish unselfishness," because such a person's "caring" is based on subconscious self-interest. At the other end ("don't give a damn") is a person who has little regard for others, who only "looks out for number one." In the middle is a kind of balance—a combination of concern for others and the obligation to take care of one's own needs as well. A person whose compassion trait resides in this middle zone recognizes that only by taking care of his own important needs first can he hope to help others, a kind of "unselfish selfishness."

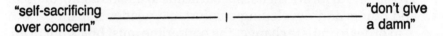

"self-sacrificing over concern" ——————— | ——————— "don't give a damn"

Figure 5-2: The "caring for others" personality trait line

Change occurs when one acquires the awareness to objectively place oneself on the spectrum and then compensate by adjusting behavior in a direction toward the middle. An individual who realistically locates his present position to the left of the midpoint would try to say "no" more often and generally attempt to be more assertive. One who places himself to the right of the midpoint would compensate toward the middle by choosing a course of action that is more sensitive to the needs of others.

Practicing Change

True change requires more than experimenting with isolated attempts to alter automatic reflexes; it involves replacing old behaviors with new ones that eventually become as natural and comfortable as the old ones. It is more than quietly stealing away from the hostile dog; it is learning how to make friends with that dog and take it for a walk.

Early on, such changes are usually uncomfortable. To use an analogy, a tennis player may decide that his unreliable backhand is in need of refinement. So he embarks on a series of tennis lessons. The new techniques that he learns to improve his game initially yield poor results. The new style is not as comfortable as his old stroke. He is tempted to revert to his previous technique. Only after continuous practice is he able to eradicate his prior bad habits and adopt the more effective and eventually more comfortable new reflexes. Likewise, psychological change requires the adoption of new reflexes to replace old ones. Only after persistent practice can such a substitution effectively, comfortably, and, therefore, permanently occur.

Learning How to Limp

Change is a monumental struggle for the borderline, much more difficult than for others because of the unique features of the disorder. Splitting and the lack of object constancy (see Chapter 2) combine to form a menacing barricade against trusting oneself and others and developing comfortable relationships.

In order to initiate change, the borderline must break out of an impossible Catch-22 position: To accept himself and others, he must learn to trust; but to trust others means to accept their consistency and dependability—quite a task for someone who, like a small child, believes others "disappear" when they leave the room. "When I can't see you," said Elizabeth to her psychiatrist early in her treatment, "it's like you don't exist."

Like someone with an injured leg, the borderline must learn to limp. If he remains bedridden, his leg muscles will atrophy and contract; if he tries to exercise too vigorously, he will reinjure the leg even more severely. Instead, he must learn to limp on it—putting just enough weight on the leg to build strength gradually, but not so much as to strain it and prevent healing. Likewise, healing in the borderline requires placing just enough pressure by challenging himself to move forward.

Leaving the Past Behind

The borderline's view of the world, like that of most people, is shaped by his childhood experiences in which the family served as a microcosm of the universe. Unlike healthier individuals, however, the borderline cannot easily separate himself from other family members, nor can he separate his family from the rest of the world.

Unable to see his world through adult eyes, the borderline

continues to experience life as a child—with a child's intense emotions and perspective. When a young child is punished or reprimanded, he sees himself as unquestionably bad; he cannot conceive of the possibility that mother might be having a bad day. As the healthy child matures, he sees his expanding world as more complex and less dogmatic. But the borderline remains stuck—a child in an adult's body.

"There is always one moment in childhood when the door opens and lets in the future," wrote Graham Greene in *The Power and the Glory*. In most borderlines' childhoods, the responsibilities of adulthood arrive too early; the door opens ever more widely but he cannot face the light. Or perhaps it is the unrelenting opening that makes facing it so difficult.

Change for the borderline comes when he learns to see current experiences—and review past memories—through adult "lenses." The new "vision" is akin to watching an old horror film on TV that you haven't seen in years: The movie, once so frightening on the big screen, seems tame—even silly—on a small screen with the lights on; you can't fathom why you were so scared when you saw it the first time.

When Elizabeth was well into her journey in psychotherapy, she began to look at her early childhood feelings in a different light. She began to accept them, to recognize the value of her own experience; if not for those early feelings and experiences, she realized, she would not have been able to bring the same fervor and motivation she was bringing to her new career in law. "Feelings born in my childhood," she said, "still continue to haunt me. But I'm even seeing that in a different light. The very ways I have hated I now accept as part of me."

Playing the Dealt Hand

The borderline's greatest obstacle to change is her tendency to evaluate in absolute extremes. The borderline must either be totally perfect or a complete failure; she grades herself either an "A+" or, more commonly, an "F." Rather than learning from the "F," she wears it like a scarlet letter and so makes the same mistakes again and again, oblivious to the patterns of her own behavior, patterns from which she could learn and grow.

Unwilling to play the hand that is dealt her, the borderline keeps folding every time, losing the ante, waiting to be dealt four aces. If she cannot be assured of winning, she won't play out the hand. Improvement comes when she learns to accept the hand for what it is, and recognize that, skillfully played, she can still win.

The borderline is sometimes paralyzed by indecisiveness. Various alternatives seem overwhelming and the borderline feels incapable of making any decisions. But as she matures, choices appear less frightening and may even become a source of pride and growing independence. At that point the borderline recognizes that she faces decisions which only she is capable of making. "I'm finding," Elizabeth noted, "that the roots of my indecisiveness are the beginning of success. I mean, the agony of choosing is that I suddenly see choices."

BOUNDARY SETTING: ESTABLISHING AN IDENTITY

One of the borderline's primary goals is to establish a separate sense of identity and to overcome the proclivity to merge with others. In biological terms, it is like advancing from a parasitic life form to a state of symbiosis and even independence. Either symbiosis or independence can be terrifying, and most border- lines find that relying on themselves is like walking for the first time.

In biology the parasite's existence is entirely dependent on the host organism. If the parasitic tick sucks too much blood from the dog, the dog dies and, thus, so does the tick. Human rela- tionships function best when they are less parasitic and more symbiotic. In symbiosis two organisms thrive better together, but may subsist independently. For example, moss growing on a tree may help the tree by shading it from direct sunlight, and help itself by having access to the tree's large supply of un- derground water. But if either the moss or the tree dies, the other may continue to survive, though less well. The borderline some- times functions as a parasite whose demanding dependence may eventually destroy the person to whom he so strongly clings; when this person leaves, the borderline may be de- stroyed. If he can learn to establish more collaborative rela- tionships with others, all may learn to live more contentedly.

Elizabeth's increasing comfort with others started with her relationship with her psychiatrist. After months of testing his loyalty by berating and criticizing him and threatening to terminate therapy, Elizabeth began to trust his commitment to her. She began to accept his flaws and mistakes, rather than see them as proof of the inevitability of his failing her. After a while, Elizabeth began to extend the developing trust between her therapist and herself to others in her life. And she began to accept herself, imperfections and all, just as she was accepting others the same way.

As Elizabeth continued to improve, she became more confident that she would not lose her "inner core." Where once she would squirm in a group of people, feeling self-conscious and out of place, she could now feel comfortable with others, letting them take responsibility for themselves and she for herself. Where once she felt compelled to adopt a role in order to fit into the group, she could now hold on to her more constant, immutable sense of self; now, she could "stay the same color" more easily.

Establishment of a constant identity means the ability to stand alone without relying on someone else to lean upon. It means trusting one's own judgment and instincts and then acting rather than waiting for the feedback of others and then reacting.

BUILDING RELATIONSHIPS

As the borderline forges a distinct core sense of identity, he also differentiates himself from others. Change requires an appreciation of others as independent persons and an empathy to understand their struggles. Their flaws and imperfections must not only be acknowledged but also understood as separate from the borderline himself.

The borderline must learn to integrate the positive and negative aspects of other individuals. When the borderline wants to get close to another person, he must learn to be independent enough to be dependent in comfortable, not desperate, ways. He learns to function symbiotically, not parasitically. The healing borderline develops a constancy about himself and about others; trust—of others and of his own perceptions—develops. The world becomes more balanced, more in-between.

Just as in climbing a mountain, the fullest experience comes when the climber can appreciate all the vistas: to look up and keep his goal firmly in view; to look down and recognize his progress as he proceeds. And finally, to rest, look around, and admire the view from right where he is at the moment. Part of the experience is recognizing that no one ever reaches the pinnacle; life is a continuous climb up the mountain. A good deal of mental health is being able to appreciate the journey—to be able to accept the reality of the Serenity Prayer of Saint Francis of Assisi: "God grant me the serenity to accept the things I cannot change, the courage to change the things I can, and the wisdom to know the difference."

Recognizing the Effect of Change on Others

When an individual first enters therapy, he often does not understand that it is "he," not others, who must make changes. However, when he does make changes, important people in his life must also adjust. Stable relationships are dynamic, fluctuating systems that have attained a state of equilibrium. When one person in that system makes significant changes in his ways of relating, others must adjust in order to recapture homeostatis, or the state of balance. If these readjustments do not occur, the system may collapse and the relationships may shatter.

For example, a woman consults a psychotherapist for severe depression and anxiety. In therapy, she rails against her alcoholic husband, whom she blames for her feelings of worthlessness. Eventually she recognizes her own role in the crumbling marriage—her own need to have others become dependent upon her, and her fears of reaching for independence. She begins to blame her husband less. She develops new, independent interests and relationships. She stops her crying episodes; she stops initiating fights over his drinking; the equilibrium of the marriage is altered.

The husband may now find that the situation is much more uncomfortable than it was before. He escalates his drinking in an unconscious attempt to reestablish the old equilibrium and have his wife return to her martyred, caretaking role. He accuses her of seeing other men and tries to disrupt their relationship, now intolerable to him.

Or, he too can begin to see the necessity for change and his own responsibility in maintaining this pathological equilibrium. He may take the opportunity to see his own actions more clearly, and reevaluate his own life, just as he has seen his wife do. Participation in therapy may be a valuable experience for everyone affected.

The more interesting and knowledgeable Elizabeth became, the more ignorant her husband seemed to her. The more opened-minded she became—the more gray she was able to perceive in a situation—the more black and white he became in order to reestablish equilibrium.

She felt that she was "leaving someone behind." That person was her—or, more closely, a part of her she no longer needed or wanted. She was, in her words, "growing up."

As Elizabeth's treatment wound down, she met less regularly with her doctor, yet still had to contend with other important people in her life. She fought with her brother, who refused to own up to his drug problem. He accused her of being "uppity," of "using her new psychological crap as ammunition." They argued bitterly over the lack of communication within the family. He told her that even after all the "shrinks," she was still "screwed up." She fought with her mother, who remained demanding, complaining, and incapable of showing her any love. She contended with her husband, who professed his love but continued to drink heavily and criticize her desire to pursue her education. He refused to help with their son and after a while she suspected his frequent absences were related to an affair with another woman.

Finally, Elizabeth began to recognize that she did not have the power to change others. She began to accept them for who they were, love them as best she could, and go on with her own life. She recognized the need for new friends and new activities in her life. Elizabeth called this "going home."

6

Communicating with the Borderline

"Alright . . . what do you want me to say? Do you want me to say it's funny, so you can contradict me and say it's sad? Or do you want me to say it's sad so you can turn around and say no, it's funny. You can play that damn little game any way you want to, you know!"
—*From* Who's Afraid of Virginia Woolf?
by Edward Albee

CONFRONTING BORDERLINE BEHAVIOR is problematic for everyone in regular contact with the borderline personality because, as we have seen, their explosions of anger, rapid mood swings, suspiciousness, impulsive actions, unpredictable outbursts, self-destructive actions and inconsistent communications are upsetting to everyone around them.

In this chapter we will describe a consistent, structured method of communicating with borderlines—the SET system—that can be easily understood and adopted by family, friends, and therapists for use on a daily basis, and which may even help in convincing a borderline to consider treatment (see Chapter 7).

Developed by the staff of the Comprehensive Treatment Unit

of Saint John's Mercy Medical Center in St. Louis, the SET system evolved as a structured framework of communication with the borderline in crisis. During such times, communication with the borderline is hindered by his impenetrable, chaotic internal force field, characterized by three major feeling states: terrifying aloneness, feelings of being misunderstood, and overwhelming helplessness.

As a result, concerned individuals are often unable to reason calmly with the borderline and instead are forced to confront outbursts of rage, impulsive destructiveness, self-harming threats or gestures, and unreasonable demands for caretaking. SET responses can serve to address the underlying fears, dilute the borderline conflagration, and prevent a "meltdown" into greater conflict.

Although SET was developed for the borderline in crisis, it can also be useful for others who require concise, consistent communication, even when not in crisis.

SET COMMUNICATION

"SET"—Support Empathy Truth—is a three-part system of communication. During confrontations of destructive behavior, important decision-making sessions, or other crises, interactions with the borderline should invoke all three of these elements.

The "S" stage of this system, "Support," invokes a personal statement of concern. "I am sincerely worried about how you are feeling" is an example of a Support statement. The emphasis is on the speaker's own feelings and is essentially a personal pledge to try to be of help.

With the "Empathy" segment, one attempts to acknowledge the borderline's chaotic feelings: "How awful you must be feeling . . . ." It is important not to confuse Empathy with sympathy ("I feel so sorry for you . . . ."), which may elicit rage over perceived condescension. Also, Empathy should be expressed in a neutral way with minimal personal reference to the speaker's own feelings. The emphasis here is on the borderline's painful experience, not the speaker's. A statement like "I know just how bad you are feeling" invites a mocking rejoinder that, indeed, you do not know, and only aggravates conflict.

The "T" statement, representing "Truth" or reality, emphasizes that the borderline is ultimately responsible for his life and that others' attempts to help cannot preempt this primary responsibility. While Support and Empathy are subjective statements acknowledging how the principals feel, Truth statements show recognition that a problem exists and address the practical issue of what can be done to solve it. "Well, what are you going to do about it?" is one essential Truth response. Other characteristic Truth expressions refer to actions that the speaker feels compelled to take in response to the borderline's behaviors, which should be expressed in a matter-of-fact, neutral fashion ("Here's what happened . . . . These are the consequences . . . . This is what I can do . . . . What are you going to do?"). But they should be stated in a way that avoids blaming and sadistic punishing ("This is a fine mess you've gotten us into!" "You made your bed; now lie in it!"). The Truth part of the "SET" system is the most important and the most difficult for the borderline to accept since so much of his world excludes or rejects realistic consequences.

Communication with the borderline should attempt to include all three messages. However, even if all three parts are stated, the borderline may not integrate all of them. Predictable responses result when one of these levels is either not clearly stated or is not "heard."

For example, when the Support stage of this system is bypassed, the borderline characteristically accuses the other of not caring or not wanting to be involved with him. The borderline then tends to tune out further exchanges on the basis that the other person does not care, or may even wish him harm. The accusation from a borderline that, "You don't care!" usually suggests that the Support statement is not being integrated.

The inability to communicate the Empathy part of the message leads to feelings that the other person does not understand what the borderline is going through. ("You don't know how I feel.") Here, the borderline will justify his rejection of the communication by saying he is misunderstood. Since the other person cannot appreciate the pain, his responses can be devalued. When either the Support or the Empathy overtures are not accepted by the borderline, further communications are not heard.

When the Truth element is not clearly expressed, a more dangerous situation emerges. The borderline interprets others' acquiescence in ways he finds most comfortable for his needs, usually as confirmation that others really can be responsible for him, or that his own perceptions are universally shared and supported. The borderline's fragile merger with these other people eventually disintegrates when the relationship is unable to sustain the weight of his unrealistic expectations. Without clearly stated Truth and confrontation, the borderline continues to be overly entangled with others. His needs gratified, the borderline will insist that all is well or, at least, that things will get better. Indeed, the evidence for this enmeshment is often a striking, temporary absence of conflict: the borderline will exhibit less hostility and anger. However, when his unrealistic expectations are eventually frustrated, the relationship collapses in a fiery maelstrom of anger and disappointment.

BORDERLINE DILEMMAS

The SET principles can be used in a variety of settings in attempts to defuse unstable situations. Following are some typical borderline predicaments in which the SET strategy may be used.

Damned If You Do, and Damned If You Don't

Borderline confusion often results in contradictory messages to others. Frequently, the borderline will communicate one position with words, but express a contradictory message with behavior. Although the borderline may not be consciously aware of this dilemma, he frequently places a friend or relation in a no-win situation in which the other person is condemned no matter which way he goes.

Case 1: Gloria and Alex. Gloria tells her husband Alex that she is forlorn and depressed. She says she plans to kill herself but forbids him from seeking help for her.

In this situation, Alex is confronted with two contradictory messages: 1. Gloria's overt message, which essentially states, "If you care about me, you will respect my wishes and not challenge my autonomy to control my own destiny and even die, if I choose," and 2. the opposite message, conveyed in the very act of announcing her intentions, which says, "For God's sake, if you care about me, help me, and don't let me die."

If Alex ignores Gloria's statements, she will accuse him of being cold and uncaring. If he attempts to list reasons why she should not kill herself, she will frustrate him with relentless counter-arguments and will ultimately condemn him for not truly understanding her pain. If he calls the police or her doctor, he will be rejecting her requests and proving that she cannot trust him.

Because Gloria doesn't feel strong enough to take responsibility for her own life, she looks to Alex to take on this burden. She feels overwhelmed and helpless in the wake of her depression. By drawing Alex into this drama, she is making him a character in her own scripted play, with an uncertain ending to be resolved not by herself, but by Alex. She faces her ambivalence about suicide by turning over to him the responsibility for what will happen to her.

Further, Gloria splits off the negative portions of her available choices and projects them onto Alex, preserving for herself the positive side of the ambivalence. No matter how Alex responds, he will be criticized. If he does not actively intercede, he is uncaring and heartless and she is "tragically misunderstood." If he tries to stop her suicide attempts, he is controlling and insensitive, while she is bereft of her self-respect.

Either way, Gloria envisions herself a helpless and self-righteous martyr—a victim who has been deprived by Alex of achieving her full potential. As for Alex, he is damned if he does and damned if he doesn't!

SET principles may be helpful in confronting a difficult situation like this. Ideally, Alex's responses should embrace all three sides of the SET triangle.

Alex's "S" statement should be a declaration of his commitment to Gloria and his wish to help her. If they can identify the specific areas of concern that are adding to her anguish, he could suggest solutions or proclaim his willingness to help: "I am very concerned about how bad you are feeling and want to help because I love you. I think some of this might be related to the problems you've been having with your boss. Let's discuss some of the alternatives. Maybe you could ask for a transfer. Or if the job is causing you this much difficulty, I want you to know that it's okay with me if you want to quit and look for another job."

The "E" statement should attempt to convey Alex's awareness of Gloria's current pain and his understanding of how such extreme circumstances might lead her to contemplate ending her life: "The pressure you've been under these past several months must be getting unbearable. All of this agony must be bringing you to the edge, to a point where you feel like you just can't go on any more."

The most important part of Alex's "T" statement should identify his untenable "damned-if-he-does and damned-if-he-doesn't" dilemma. He should also attempt to clarify Gloria's ambivalence about dying by acknowledging that in addition to that part of her that wants to end her life, another part of her wishes to be saved and helped. Alex's "T" responses might be something like: "I recognize how bad you are feeling and your wish to die. I know you said that if I cared at all for you, I should just leave you alone. But if I cared, how could I possibly sit back and watch you destroy yourself? Your telling me about your suicidal plans tells me that, as much as you wish to die, there is at least some part of you that doesn't want to die. And it is to that part that I feel I must respond. I want you to come with me to see a doctor to help us with these problems."

Depending on the immediacy of the circumstances, Alex should insist that Gloria be psychiatrically evaluated soon or, if she is in imminent danger, he should take her to an emergency room or seek help from police or paramedics.

At this juncture Gloria's fury may be exacerbated as she blames Alex for forcing her into the hospital. But Truth statements should remind Gloria that she is there not so much because of what Alex did, but because of what Gloria did—threatening suicide. The borderline may frequently need to be reminded that others' reactions to him are based primarily on what *he* does, and that *he* must take responsibility for the consequences, rather than blaming others for realistic responses to his behavior.

When the immediate danger has passed, subsequent "T" statements should refer to Gloria's unproductive patterns of handling stress and the need to develop more effective ways of dealing with her life. Truth considerations should also include how Gloria's and Alex's behaviors affect each other and their marriage. Over time they may be able to work out a system of responding to each other, either on their own or within therapy, that will fulfill the needs of both.

This kind of problem is especially common within families of borderlines who display prominent self-destructive behaviors. Delinquent or suicidal adolescents, alcoholics, and anorexics may present similar no-win dilemmas to their families. They actively resist help, while behaving in obviously self-destructive ways. Usually, direct confrontation that precipitates a crisis is the only way to help. Some groups, such as Alcoholics Anonymous, recommend standardized confrontational situations in which family, friends, or coworkers, together with a counselor, confront the patient with his addictive behavior and demand treatment.

"Tough Love" groups believe that true caring is forcing the individual to face the consequences of his behaviors rather than protecting him from them. Tough Love groups for parents of teenagers, for example, may insist that an adolescent drug abuser either be hospitalized or barred from the home. This type of approach emphasizes the Truth element of the SET triangle but may ignore the Support and Empathy segments. Therefore, these systems may be only partially successful for the borderline, who may go through the motions of change that Truth confrontations force on him; underneath, however, the lack of nurturing and trust provided by Support and Empathy hinder his motivation for dedicated and lasting change.

Feeling Bad About Feeling Bad

Borderlines typically respond to depression, anxiety, frustration, or anger with more layers of these same feelings. Because of the borderline's perfectionism and tendency to perceive things in black-and-white extremes, he attempts to obliterate unpleasant feelings rather than understand or cope with them. When he finds that he cannot simply erase these bad feelings, he becomes even more frustrated or guilty. Since feeling bad is unacceptable, he feels bad about feeling bad. When this makes him feel worse, he becomes caught in a seemingly bottomless downward spiral.

One of the goals for the borderline's therapists and other close relations is to crack through these successive layers to locate the original feeling and help the borderline accept it as part of himself. The borderline must learn to allow himself the luxury of "bad" feelings without rebuke, guilt, or denial.

Case 2: Neil and Friends. Neil, a fifty-three-year-old bank officer, has had episodes of depression for more than half his life. Neil's parents died when he was young, and he was reared mostly by his much older and unmarried sister, who was cold and hypercritical. She was a religious zealot who insisted he attend church services daily, and frequently accused him of sinful transgressions.

Neil grew up to become a passive man, dominated by his wife. He was reared to believe that anger was unacceptable and denied ever feeling angry at others. He was hard-working and respected at his job, but received little affection from his wife. She rejected his sexual advances, which frustrated and depressed him. Neil would initially get angry at his wife for her rejections, then feel guilty and get angry at himself for being angry, and then lapse into depression. This process permeated other areas of Neil's life. Whenever he experienced negative feelings, he would pressure himself to end them. Since he could not control his inner feelings, he became increasingly disappointed and frustrated with himself. His depression worsened.

Neil's friends tried to comfort him. They told him they were behind him and were available whenever he wanted to talk. They empathized with his discomfort at work and his problems in dealing with his wife. They pointed out that "he was feeling bad over feeling bad," and that he should straighten up. This advice, however, didn't help; in fact, Neil felt worse because he now felt he was letting his friends down on top of everything else. The harder he tried to stop his negative feelings, the more he felt like a failure, and the more depressed he became.

SET statements could help Neil confront this dilemma. Neil received much Support and Empathy from his friends, but their Truth messages were not helpful. Rather than trying to erase his unpleasant emotions (an all-or-none proposition), Neil must understand the necessity of accepting them as real and appropriate.

Further Truth statements would acknowledge the reasons for Neil's passive behavior and the behaviors of his wife and others in his life. He must recognize that, to some degree, he places himself in a position of being abused by others. Although he can work to change this situation in the future, he must now deal with the way things are currently. This means recognizing his anger, that he has reasons to be angry, and that he has no choice but to accept his anger, for he cannot make it disappear, at least not right away. Though he may regret the presence of unacceptable feelings, he is powerless to change them (a dictum similar to those used by Alcoholics Anonymous). Accepting these uncomfortable feelings means accepting himself as an imperfect human being and relinquishing the illusion that he can control uncontrollable factors. If Neil can accept his anger, or his sadness, or any unpleasant feeling, the "feeling bad about feeling bad" phenomenon will be short-circuited. He can move on to change other aspects of his life.

The borderline trapped in this dilemma will often break free when he least expects it—when he relaxes, becomes less obsessive and self-demanding, and learns to accept himself. It is no coincidence that the borderline who seeks a healthy love relationship more often finds it when he is least desperate for one and more engaged in self-fulfilling activities. For it is at this point that he is more attractive to others and less pressured to grasp at immediate and unrealistic solutions to loneliness.

The Perennial Victim

The borderline frequently involves himself in predicaments in which he becomes a victim. Neil, for example, perceives himself as a helpless character upon whom others act. The borderline frequently is unaware that his behavior is provocative or dangerous, or that it may in some way invite persecution. The woman who continually chooses men who abuse her is typically unaware of the patterns she is repeating. The borderline's split view of himself includes a special, entitled part and an angry, unworthy part that masochistically deserves punishment, although he may not be consciously aware of one side or the other. In fact, a pattern of this type of "invited" victimization is often a solid indication of BPD pathology.

Although being a victim is most unpleasant, it can also be a very appealing role. A helpless waif, buffeted by the turbulent seas of an unfair world, is very attractive to some people. A match between the helpless waif and one who feels a strong need to rescue and take care of others satisfies needs for both parties. The borderline finds a "kind stranger" who promises complete and total protection. And the partner fulfills his own desire to feel strong, protective, important, and needed—to be the one to "take him away from all this."

Case 3: Annette. Born to a poor black family, Annette lost her father at a very young age when he abandoned the family. A succession of other men briefly occupied the "father" chair in the home. Eventually her mother remarried, but her second husband was also a drinker and carouser. When Annette was about eight, her stepfather began sexually abusing her and her sister. Annette was afraid to tell her mother, who gloried in the family's finally achieving some financial security. So Annette allowed it to continue—for her mother's sake.

At seventeen, Annette became pregnant and married the baby's father. She managed to graduate from high school, where her grades were generally good, but other aspects of her life were in turmoil: Her husband drank and ran with other women. After awhile, he began beating her. She continued to bear more of his children, complaining and enduring—for the children's sake.

After six years and three children, Annette's husband left her. His departure prompted a kind of anxious relief—the wild ride was finally over, but concerns over what to do next loomed ominously.

Annette and the kids tried to make things work, but she felt constantly overwhelmed. Then she met John, who was about twenty-five years older (he refused to tell her his exact age) and seemed to have a genuine desire to take care of her. He became the good father Annette never had. He encouraged and protected her. He advised her on how to dress and how to talk. After awhile, Annette became more self-confident, got a good job, and began enjoying her life. A few months later, John moved in—sort of. He lived with her on weekends but slept away during the week because of work assignments that made it "more convenient to sleep at the office."

Deep inside, Annette knew John was married, but she never asked. When John became less dependable, stayed away more and generally became more detached, she held in her anger. On the job, however, this anger surfaced, and she was passed over for many promotions. Her supervisors said that she lacked the academic qualifications of others and that she was abrasive sometimes, but Annette wouldn't accept those explanations.

Incensed, she attributed the rejections to racial discrimination. She became more and more depressed and eventually entered the hospital.

In the hospital, Annette's racial sensitivities exploded. Most of the doctors were white, as were most of the nurses and most of the other patients. The hospital decor was "white" and the meals were "white." All of the anger built up over the years was now focused on society's discrimination against blacks. By concentrating exclusively on this global issue, Annette avoided her own personal demons.

Her most challenging target was Harry, a music therapist on staff at the hospital. Annette felt that Harry (who was white) insisted on playing only "white" music, and that his looks and whole demeanor embodied "whiteness." Annette vented her fury on this therapist, and she would stalk away angrily from the music therapy sessions.

Although Harry was frightened by the outbursts, he sought out Annette. His Support statement reflected his personal concern about Annette's progress in the hospital program. Harry expressed his Empathy for Annette by voicing his recognition of how frustrating it feels to be discriminated against, and cited his own experiences as one of the only Jews in his educational program. Then Harry attempted to confront the Truth, or reality, issues in Annette's life, pointing out that railing against racial discrimination was useless without a commitment to work toward changing it. Annette's need to remain a victim, Harry said, shielded her from assuming any responsibility for what happened in her life. She could feel justified in cursing the fates rather than bravely investigating her own role in continuing to be used by others. By wrapping herself in a veil of righteous anger, Annette was avoiding any kind of frightening self-examination or confrontation that might induce change, and thereby was perpetuating her impotency and helplessness.

At the next music therapy session, Annette did not stalk out of the room. Instead, she berated Harry and the other patients. She suggested different songs to play. At the following meeting the group agreed to play some civil-rights protest songs of Annette's choosing.

Harry's response exemplified SET principles and would have been useful for Annette's boss, her friends—anyone who faced her angry outbursts on a regular basis.

SET communication can free a borderline or anyone who is locked into a victim role by pointing out the advantages of being a victim (being cared for, appearing blameless for bad results, disavowing responsibility) and the disadvantages (abdicating autonomy, maintaining obsequious dependency, remaining fixated and immobile amidst life's dilemmas). The borderline "victim" must, however, hear all three parts of the message; otherwise the impact of the message will be lost. If "the Truth will set you free," then Support and Empathy must accompany it to insure it will be heard.

Quest for Meaning

Much of the borderline's dramatic behavior is related to his interminable search for something to fill the emptiness that continually haunts him. Relationships and drugs are two of the mechanisms the borderline uses to beat the loneliness and to capture a sense of existing in a world that feels real.

Case 4: Rich. "I guess I just love too much!" said Rich in describing his problems with his girlfriend. He was a thirty-year-old divorced man who experienced a succession of disastrous affairs with women. He would cling obsessively to these women, showering them with gifts and attention. Through them he felt whole, alive, and fulfilled. But he demanded from them—and from other friends—total obedience. In this way he felt in control, not only of them but more importantly of his own existence.

He became distraught when these women acted independently. He cajoled, insisted, and threatened. To stave off the omnipresent sense of emptiness, he attempted to control others; if they refused to comply with his wishes, Rich became seriously depressed and out of control. He would turn to alcohol or drugs to recapture his sense of being or authenticity. Sometimes he would pick fights or cut himself when he feared he was losing touch with his sensory or emotional feelings. When the anger and pain no longer brought changes, he would take up with another woman who perceived him as "misunderstood" and merely needing "the love of a good woman." Then the process would start all over again.

Rich lacked insight into his dilemma, insisting that it was

always "the bitches' fault." He dismissed his friends as not caring or not understanding—they were not able to convey Support or Empathy. The women he became involved with were initially sympathetic, but lacked the Truth component. Rich needed to be confronted with all three aspects.

In this situation, the "S" message would convey caring about Rich. The "E" part would accept without challenge Rich's feeling of "loving too much" but would also help him understand his sense of emptiness and his need to fill it.

The Truth message would attempt to point out the patterns in Rich's life that seem to repeat endlessly. Truth should also help Rich see that he uses women as he does drugs and self-mutilation—as objects or maneuvers to relieve numbness and feel whole. As long as Rich continues to search outside himself for inner contentment, he will remain frustrated and disappointed, because he cannot control outside forces and especially others, as he can control himself. For instance, despite his most frenzied efforts to regulate her, a new girlfriend will retain some independence outside the realm of Rich's control. Or, he could lose a new job due to economic factors that may eliminate the position. But Rich *can* control his own creative powers, intellectual curiosity, and so on. Independent personal interests—books, hobbies, arts, sports—can serve as reliable and enduring sources of satisfaction, which cannot easily be taken away.

Search for Constancy

Adjusting to a world that is continually inconsistent and untrustworthy is a major problem for the borderline. The borderline's universe lacks pattern and predictability. Friends, jobs, and skills can never be relied upon. The borderline must keep testing and retesting all of these aspects of his life; he is in constant fear that a trusted person or situation will change into its total opposite—absolute betrayal. A hero becomes a devil; the perfect job becomes the bane of his existence.

Case 5: Pat and Jake. Pat was an attractive twenty-nine-year-old woman in the process of divorcing her second husband. As with her first husband, she accused him of being an alcoholic and of abusing her. Her lawyer, Jake, saw her as an unfortunate victim in need of protection. He called her frequently to be sure she was all right. They began to have lunch together. As the case proceeded, they became lovers. Jake moved out of his house and away from his wife and two sons. Though not yet divorced, Pat moved in with him.

At first, Pat admired Jake's intelligence and expertise. Where she felt weak and defenseless, he seemed "big and strong." But over time she became increasingly demanding. As long as Jake was protective, Pat cooed. But when he began to make demands, she became hostile. She resented his going to work and particularly his involvement in other divorce cases. She resisted his visits to his children and accused him of choosing them over her. She would initiate brutal fights, which often culminated in her rushing out of the house to spend the night with a male "platonic friend."

Pat lacked object constancy (see Chapter 2 and Appendix B). Friendships and love relationships had to be constantly tested because she never felt secure with any human contact. Her need for reassurance was insatiable. She had been through countless other relationships in which she first appeared ingenuous and in need of caretaking and then tested them with outrageous demands. The relationships all ended with precisely the abandonment she feared; then she would repeat the process in her next romance.

At first, when Pat perceived Jake as supportive and reassuring, she idealized their relationship. But when he exhibited signs of functioning separately, she became enraged, cursing and denigrating him. When he was at the office, she would call him incessantly because, as she said, she was "forgetting him." To her friends, Jake sounded like two completely different people—for Pat, he was.

SET confrontations of object inconstancy require recognition of this borderline dilemma. Support statements must convey that caring is constant, unconditional. Unfortunately, the borderline personality, or Pat in this case, has difficulty grasping that she does not need to earn acceptance continuously. She is in constant fear that Support could be withdrawn if at any point she displeases.

The Empathy message should confirm an understanding that Pat has not yet learned to trust Jake's attempts at reassurance. Jake tries to communicate his awareness of the horrific anxieties Pat is experiencing and how frightening it is for her to be alone.

Truth declarations must include attempts to reconcile the split parts. Jake has to explain that he cares for Pat all the time, even when he is frustrated by her. He must also declare his intention not to allow himself to be abused. Capitulation to Pat's demands will only result in more demands. Trying to please and satisfy Pat is an impossible task, for it is never finished—new insecurities will always arise. Truth will probably mandate ongoing therapy for both of them, if their relationship is to continue.

The Rage of Innocence

Borderline rage is often terrifying in its unpredictability and intensity. It may be sparked by relatively insignificant events and appear without warning. It may be directed at previously valued people. The threat of violence frequently accompanies this anger. All of these features make borderline rage much different from typical anger.

In an instant, Pat could transform from a docile, dependent, childlike woman into a demanding, screaming harpy. On one occasion she suggested that she and Jake have a quiet lunch together. But when Jake told her he had to go to the office, she suddenly began screaming at him, inches from his face, accusing him of being inconsiderate of her needs. She viciously attacked his manhood, his failures as a husband and father, and his profession. She threatened to report him to the Bar Association for misconduct. When Jake's attempts to placate her failed, he would silently leave the scene, which infuriated Pat even more. But when he returned, both would act as if nothing had ever happened.

SET principles must first of all address safety issues. Volatility must be contained. In the scenario above, Jake's Support and Empathy messages should come first, though Pat will probably reject them as insincere. In such cases it is imprudent for Jake to continue to argue that he cares and understands that she is upset. He must move immediately to Truth statements, which must first declare that no one will be hurt. He must firmly tell her to back off, to allow some physical distance. He can inform her of his wish to communicate calmly with her. If she will not allow this, he can state his intention of leaving until the situation quiets down, at which point they can resume discussions. He must try to avoid physical conflict, despite Pat's provocations.

Although unconsciously Pat may actually want Jake to physically overpower her, this need is based on unhealthy experiences
from her past, and will likely later be used to criticize him more.

Truth statements made during angry confrontations are often
better directed toward the underlying dynamics than toward the
specifics of the clash. Further debate about whether taking Pat to
lunch is more important than going to the office will probably be
unproductive. However, Jake might address Pat's apparent
need to fight and her possible wish to be overpowered and hurt.
He might also confront Pat's behavior as a need to be rejected. Is
she so fearful of anticipating rejection that she is precipitating it
in order to "hurry up and get it over with"? The primary Truth
message is that this behavior is driving Jake away. He may ask if
this is really what Pat wants.

Fatal Attraction

In the movie *Fatal Attraction*, Dan Gallager is a happily married
man who engages in a tempestuous affair with Alex Forrest, an
attractive, apparently successful career woman. Though the film
does not explore Alex's character in depth, it is obvious that the
filmmakers had several borderline traits in mind when creating
the role. Alex has few (if any) friends and a history of several job
changes. When Dan attempts to terminate the relationship, Alex
becomes enraged at being abandoned and panicked at the
thought of being alone. From a sophisticated, carefree seduc-
tress she changes into a clinging, dependent, suicidal child. In
desperation, she impulsively cuts her wrists and manipulates
Dan into staying with her.

From this point, the film moves through a series of dramatic
and sometimes violent confrontations between Alex, Dan, and
Dan's wife, Beth. The film's story of an apparent borderline
personality's descent into madness—and how others dealt with
it—must have touched some kind of chord of recognition in the
American public for the movie was one of the biggest box office
successes of 1987 and the most popular video rental of 1988.

In a sense, the film itself was a borderline creation in its
Hollywood portrayal of black-and-white "good guys" and "bad
guys": Alex was portrayed as a stereotype "evil villainess,"
rather than a complex, anguished, mentally ill woman; Dan was
the "good husband who happened to stray" rather than a weak-
willed adulterer who had at least an indirect role in the ensuing

violence. It was no accident that, like old-time white-hat, black-hat westerns, the movie typically elicited cheers and boos in movie theatres.

Dan's reactions to Alex ignored basic SET principles, which inevitably led all three main characters to the film's bloody ending. The following script would not have been nearly so sensational (nor probably as successful) as the original, but might have saved everyone a great deal of anguish:

When confronted by Alex's bleeding wrists, Dan should have first expressed his Support and concern for Alex—"I am extremely shocked and upset at what you have done, and want to help you." Further Support would have included aiding in cleansing and bandaging her wounds.

His Empathy message would have reflected understanding of her anguish. "You are obviously very upset, more than I realized, and must be hurting very badly inside." Encouraging her to talk about her loneliness—what she was feeling and why—would have been helpful "E" input.

In the film, Dan—due to his own character flaws—was unable to confront the Truth side of either Alex's or his own actions, and thus became hopelessly ensnared. Truth messages would have included reminders that, even though both had had the fling as equal partners, Alex knew he was married and would return to his family. More importantly, it was Alex, not he, who was behaving self-destructively. Depending on the seriousness of Alex's cuts, he might have insisted that she seek medical attention. He would have strongly encouraged her to seek psychiatric care (while acknowledging that he could not force her to do so). He would also have admitted his role in what is clearly a destructive relationship, and the obvious need to terminate it. In all of these Truth messages, Dan would have tried to delineate the borders—between what he can do and what Alex can do.

THE NEED FOR CONSISTENCY

All Truth statements must, indeed, be true. For the borderline, already living in a world of inconsistencies, it is much worse to make idle threats about the consequences of an action than to passively allow inappropriate behaviors to continue. In *Fatal*

Attraction, Alex was used to resisting rejection by manipulating others. For Dan to say he was going to end the relationship without unequivocally doing so was destructive. Of course, he didn't know that following the termination of an intense relationship, the borderline is unable to "be just friends"—an "in-between" relationship that the borderline finds intolerable.

Because the borderline has such difficulty with equivocation, intentions must be backed up with clear, predictable actions. A parent who threatens his adolescent with revocation of privileges for certain behaviors, for example, and then does not carry out his promises, exacerbates the problem. A therapist who purports to set limits for therapy—establishing fees, limiting phone calls, etc.—but then does not follow through, invites increased borderline testing.

Borderlines are often reared in situations in which threats and dramatic actions are the only ways to achieve what is wanted. Just as the borderline perceives acceptance as conditional, so rejection can also be seen this way. The borderline feels that if only he is attractive enough, or smart enough, or rich enough, or demanding enough, he will ultimately get what he wants. The more outrageous behavior is rewarded, the more the borderline will employ such maneuvers.

Although the SET principles were developed for working with borderline patients, they can be useful for dealing with others. When communications between people are stalled, SET can help focus on messages that are not being successfully transmitted. If an individual feels that he is not supported or respected, or that he is misunderstood, or if he refuses to address realistic problems, specific SET steps can be taken to reinforce these flagging areas. In today's complex world, a clear set of communication principles that includes both love and reason are necessary to overcome the tribulations of borderline chaos.

7

Seeking Therapy

"I'm gonna give him one more year, and then I'm going to Lourdes."
—*Woody Allen, talking about his psychiatrist in* Annie Hall

DR. SMITH, A nationally-known psychiatrist, had called me about his niece. She was depressed and in need of a good psychotherapist. He was calling to say that he had recommended me.

Arranging an appointment was difficult. She could not rearrange her schedule to fit my openings. So, I juggled and rearranged my schedule to fit hers. I felt pressure to be accommodating and brilliant, so that Dr. Smith's faith in me would be justified. I had just opened my practice and desperately needed some validation of my professional skills. Yet, I knew that these feelings were a bad sign: I was nervous.

Julie was strikingly attractive. Tall and blonde, she easily could have been a model. A law student, she was twenty-five, bright, and articulate. She arrived ten minutes late and neither apologized for nor acknowledged this slight on her part. When I looked closely, I could see that her eye makeup was a little too heavy, as if she were trying to conceal a sadness and exhaustion inside.

Julie was an only child, very dependent on her successful parents, who were always travelling. Because she couldn't stand being alone, she cruised through a series of affairs. When a man would break off the relationship, she'd become extremely depressed until embarking on the next affair. She was now "between relationships." Her most recent man had left her and "there was no one to replace him."

It wasn't long before her treatment established a routine. As a session would near its end, she'd always bring up something important, so our appointments would end a little late. The phone calls between sessions became more frequent and lasted longer.

Over the next six weeks we met once a week, but then mutually agreed to increase the frequency to twice a week. She talked about her loneliness and her difficulties with separations, but continued to feel hopeless and alone. She told me that she often burst out in rage against her friends, though these outbursts were hard to imagine because she was so demure in my office. She had problems sleeping, her appetite decreased, and she was losing weight. She began to talk about suicide. I prescribed antidepressant medications for her, but she felt even more depressed and was unable to concentrate at school. Finally, after three months of treatment, I recommended hospitalization, which she reluctantly accepted. Clearly, more intense work was needed to deal with this unremitting depression.

The first time I saw the anger was the day of her admission, when Julie was describing her decision to come to the hospital. Crying softly, she spoke of the fear she had experienced when explaining her hospitalization to her father.

Then suddenly her face hardened, and she said, "Do you know what that bitch did?" A few moments passed before I realized that Julie was now referring to Irene, the nurse who had admitted her to the unit. Furiously, Julie described the nurse's lack of attention, her awkwardness with the blood pressure cuff, and a mix-up with a lunch tray. Her ethereal beauty mutated into a face of rage and terror. I jumped when she pounded the table.

After a few days, Julie was galvanizing the unit with her demands and tirades. Some of the nurses and patients tried to calm and placate her; others bristled when she threw tantrums (and objects) and walked out of group sessions.

"Do you know what *your* patient did this morning, doctor?" asked one nurse as I stepped onto the floor. The accent was clearly on the "your," as if I were responsible for Julie's behavior and deserved the staff's reprimands for not controlling her. "You're overprotective. She's manipulating you. She needs to be confronted."

I immediately came to my own—and Julie's—defense. "She needs support and caring," I replied. "She needs to be re-parented. She needs to learn trust." How dare they question my judgment! Do I dare question it?

Throughout the first week, Julie had complained about the nurses, the other patients, the other doctors. She said I was understanding and caring and I had much greater insight and knowledge than the other therapists she had seen.

Julie needed a weekend pass to run errands. The nurses were skeptical; they didn't know her well enough. She hadn't talked much about herself either to them or in group therapy. She was talking only to her doctor; but she needed the pass, so I authorized it.

She returned drunk and with scratches on her wrist. Though the nurses never actually said, "I told you so," their haughty looks were unmistakable and insufferable. I began to avoid them even more than I had until that point. I resumed Julie's therapy on an individual basis, and dropped her from group sessions.

On the following weekend she needed another pass. When I turned down the request, she exploded. "I thought you trusted me," she said. "I thought you understood me. All you care about is power. You just love to control people."

Maybe she's right, I thought. Perhaps I am too controlling, too insecure. Or was she just attacking my vulnerable areas, my need to be perceived as caring and trusting? Was she just stoking my guilt and masochism? Was she the victim here, or was I?

"I thought you were different," she said. "I thought you were special. I thought you really cared." The problem was, I thought so too.

A few weeks later, I gave her another pass. She returned, intoxicated and tearful, after a sleazy liaison with a stranger in a bar. The situation was becoming clearer to me. She was begging for limits and controls and structure, but couldn't acknowledge this dependency. So she acted outrageously to make controls necessary, and then got angry and denied her wish for them.

I could see this, but she couldn't. Gradually I stopped looking forward to seeing her. Whenever I visited her, I was reminded of my failure, and I found myself wishing that she would either get well or disappear. When she voiced the opinion that maybe her roommate's doctor would be better for her, I interpreted this as a means of running away from herself and the real issues at stake. A change would be counterproductive for her, I knew, but silently I hoped that she would change doctors for my sake. She still talked of killing herself, and I guiltily fantasized that it would be almost a relief for me if she did. Her changes had changed me from a masochist to a sadist.

During her third week in the hospital, another patient hanged himself while home on a pass. Frightened, Julie flew into a rage: "Why didn't you and the staff know he was going to kill himself?" she screamed. "How could you let him do it? Why didn't you protect him?"

Julie was devastated. Who was going to protect *her*? Who would make the pain go away? I finally realized that it would have to be Julie. No one else lived inside her skin. No one else could totally understand and protect her. It was starting to make some sense, both to me and to Julie.

She could see that no matter how hard she tried to run away from her feelings, she could not escape being herself. Even though she wanted to run away from the bad person she thought she was, she had to learn to accept herself, flaws and all. Ultimately, she would see that just being herself was okay.

Julie's anger at the staff gradually moved to the suicide victim, who "didn't give himself a chance." When she saw his responsibility, she began to see hers. She discovered that people who really cared about her did not let her do whatever she wanted, as her parents had done; sometimes caring meant setting limits. Sometimes it meant telling her what she didn't want to hear. And sometimes it meant reminding her of her accountability to herself.

It wasn't long before all of us—Julie, the staff, and I—began working together. I stopped trying so hard to be likeable, wise, and unerring; it was more important to be consistent and reliable—to *be there*.

After seven weeks, Julie left the hospital; she was still lonely and afraid, but she didn't need to hurt herself any more. Even more important, she was accepting the fact that she could survive loneliness and fear but could still care about herself.

After awhile, Julie found a new man who really seemed to care about her. As for me, I learned some of the same things as Julie did—that distasteful emotions determine who I am to a great extent and that accepting these unpleasant parts of myself helps me to better understand my patients.

Therapists who treat borderline personality often find that the rigors of treatment place a great strain on their professional abilities, as well as on their patience. Treatment sessions are stormy, frustrating, and unpredictable. The treatment period proceeds at a snail-like pace; most psychotherapists agree that effective treatment requires at least several years. More than 90 percent of borderline patients who seek therapy eventually drop out prematurely.[1]

Treatment is so difficult because the borderline responds to it in much the same way as to other personal relationships. The borderline will see the therapist as caring, capable, and honest one moment, deceitful, devious, and uncaring the next.

In therapy, the borderline can be extremely demanding, dependent, and manipulative. It's not uncommon for a borderline patient to telephone incessantly between sessions and then appear unexpectedly in the therapist's office, threatening bodily harm to himself unless the therapist meets with him immediately.

Angry tirades against the therapist and the process of therapy are common. Often, the borderline can be very perceptive about the sensitivity of the therapist and eventually goad him into anger, frustration, self-doubt, and hopelessness.

Given the wide range of possible causes of BPD, and the extremes of behavior involved, there is a predictably wide range of treatment methods: (1.) psychoanalytically-oriented psychotherapy; (2.) so-called "supportive" psychotherapy; (3.) special forms of psychotherapy, such as group, family, and expressive (art, music, dance) psychotherapy; (4.) psychopharmacological (drug) therapy; and (5.) hospital-based therapy. These methods can overlap (for example, group therapy can be exploratory or supportive). Because they have met with variable levels of success, there is wide debate within the mental health profession on the most appropriate methods of treatment.

Other forms of therapy, such as behavior modification and hypnosis, are not usually employed in treating the borderline, except in special circumstances. For carefully selected patients, hypnotherapy, for example, can be useful to help recall past traumas. However, because a trance state may induce an unstructured or unfamiliar state of consciousness, severe panic or psychosis may be precipitated in the borderline patient who is inappropriately selected for this treatment.

THE BORDERLINE ON THE COUCH

During the forties and fifties, individual psychoanalysis was considered the premier treatment for all mental illnesses. However, as the concept of the borderline personality disorder became more defined over the ensuing decades, it became increasingly clear that traditional psychoanalysis was not effective for those patients diagnosed as borderline.

In classical .psychoanalysis patients are asked to engage in "free association"—speaking freely on whatever comes to mind, without censoring thoughts, and without specific guidance from the analyst. Patients typically explore early childhood memories and associate to dreams and random thoughts.

For the borderline patient, however, such unstructured therapy can be devastating. In classical psychoanalysis, the borderline's defenses are attacked, but he lacks the resources to replace them; transference feelings toward the therapist and for others can be so intense that they take on psychotic proportions.

Analysts soon discovered that borderlines became worse "on the couch." The stimulation of analysis, which could be therapeutic for the healthier patient, produced panic in the borderline. Anxieties emerged that could not be controlled or solved. Borderline patients sometimes lost contact with reality.

Over the past thirty years the borderline syndrome has increasingly displaced other psychiatric illnesses as one of the most common maladies encountered by clinical psychiatrists. Formerly masquerading as traditional neurotics, borderline patients were initially engaged in classical psychoanalysis, which led to disastrous results. But as the shift in the psychiatric population became more widely recognized, modifications of traditional psychoanalytic techniques were developed. Such therapy adjustments may be termed "psychoanalytically-oriented" or "psychodynamic." In essence they retain the theoretical base of psychoanalysis but without the trappings.

The couch, the "silent" analyst, and free association are replaced by face-to-face communications with a more interactive therapist.

During the fifties, other treatment approaches also became more accepted. Nonanalytic individual therapies acquired their own scientific bases. Family and group techniques were recognized to have value in the treatment of a variety of mental illnesses.

The advent of the "pharmacotherapy era" brought promise of cure through drug treatments. Hospital care was evolving, providing a controlled, structured, and intensive treatment milieu that obliterated the notion of the hospital as warehousing asylum.

GOALS OF THERAPY

All treatment approaches strive for a common goal: more effective functioning in a world that is experienced as less mystifying, less harmful, and more pleasurable. The process usually involves developing insight into the unproductiveness of current behavior. This is the easy part. More difficult is the process of reworking old reflexes and developing new ways of dealing with life's stresses.

The most important part of any therapy is the relationship between the patient and therapist. This interaction forms the foundation for trust, object constancy, and emotional intimacy. The therapist must become a trusted figure, a mirror to reflect a developing, consistent identity. Starting with this relationship, the borderline learns to extend to others appropriate expectations and trust.

The primary goal of the therapist is to work toward losing (not keeping) his patient. This is accomplished by directing the patient's attention to certain areas for examination, not by controlling him. Though the therapist serves as the navigator, pointing out landscapes of interest and helping to re-route the itinerary around storm conditions, it is the patient who must remain firmly in the pilot's seat. Family and loved ones are also usually included on this journey. A major objective is for the patient to return home and improve relationships, not to abandon them.

Some people are fearful of psychiatry and psychotherapy, perceiving the process as a form of "mind control" or behavior modification perpetrated on helpless, dependent patients who are molded into robots by bearded, Svengali-like mesmerists. The aim of psychotherapy is to help a patient individuate and achieve more freedom and personal dignity. Unfortunately, just as some people erroneously believe that you can be hypnotized against your will, so some believe you can be therapized against your will. Such irrational fears may deprive people of opportunities to escape self-imposed captivity and achieve self-acceptance.

LENGTH OF THERAPY

Because of the prominence of psychoanalysis, which characteristically requires several years of treatment, most people view any form of psychotherapy as being extended and drawn out, and, therefore, very expensive. The addition of medications and specialized treatments (such as so-called "time-limited" therapy) to the therapeutic armamentarium are responses to the need for practical and affordable treatment methods. Broken bones heal and infections clear up, but scars on the psyche may require much longer treatment.

If therapy terminates quickly, one may question if it was too superficial. If it extends for many years, one may wonder if it is merely intellectual game playing that enriches psychotherapists while financially enslaving their dependent and helpless patients.

How long should therapy last? The answer depends on the specific goals. Resolution of specific, targeted symptoms—such as depression, severe anxiety, or temper outbursts—may be accomplished in relatively brief time spans, such as weeks or months. If the goal is more profound restructuring, much more time will be required.

Therapy may be interrupted. It is not unusual for borderlines to engage in several separate rounds of therapy, with different therapists and different techniques. Breaks in therapy may be useful to solidify ideas, or to try out new insights, or merely to catch up with life and allow time to grow and mature. Financial limitations, significant life changes, or just a need for a respite from the intensity of treatment may mandate a time out.

Usually, the borderline requires years of therapy, in order to achieve substantive changes in functioning. When the changes come slowly, it can be difficult to determine whether more work should proceed, or if "this is as good as it gets." The therapist must consider both the borderline's propensity to run from confrontations with his unhealthy behaviors, and his tendency to cling dependently to the therapist (and others).

For some borderlines therapy may never formally end. They may derive great benefit from continuing intermittent contacts with a trusted therapist. Such arrangements would be considered "refueling stops" on the road to greater independence, provided the patient does not rely on these contacts to drive his life.

HOW PSYCHOTHERAPY WORKS

Therapy is the process of discussing the past and present in order to discover patterns that can affect the future. Whether in an individual, group, or family setting, the therapist tries to guide clients to examine their experience and serves as a touchstone for experimenting with new behaviors. Ultimately, the patient begins to accept his own choices in life and to change his self-image as a helpless pawn moved by forces beyond his control. Much of this process emerges from the primary relationship between therapist and patient. During therapy, both develop intense feelings, called "transference" and "countertransference."

Transference

Transference refers to the patient's unrealistic projections onto the therapist of feelings and attitudes previously experienced from other important persons in the patient's life. For example, a patient may get very angry with the doctor, based not on the doctor's communications, but on feelings that the doctor is much like his mother, who in the past elicited much anger from him. By itself, transference is neither negative or positive; but it is always a distortion, a projection of past emotions onto current objects.

Borderline transference is likely to be extremely inconsistent, just like other aspects of the patient's life. The borderline will see the therapist as caring, capable, and honest one moment, deceitful, devious, and unfeeling the next. These distortions make the establishment of an alliance with the therapist most difficult. Yet establishing and sustaining this alliance is the most important part of any treatment.

In the beginning stages of therapy, the borderline both craves and fears closeness to the therapist. He wants to be taken care of but fears being overwhelmed and controlled. He attempts to seduce the doctor into taking care of him and rebels against his attempts to "control his life." As the therapist remains steadfast and consistent in withstanding his tirades, object constancy develops—the borderline begins to trust that the therapist will not abandon him. From this beachhead of trust, the borderline can venture out with new relationships and establish more trusting contacts. Initially, however, such new friendships can be difficult to sustain for the borderline who, in the past, may have learned that the formation of new alliances was disloyal. He may even fear that his mate, friend, or therapist may become jealous and enraged if he broadens his social contacts.

As the borderline progresses, he settles into a more comfortable, trusting dependency. As he prepares for termination, however, there may again be a resurgence of turmoil in the relationship. He may pine for his previous ways of functioning and resent needing to proceed onward; he may feel like a tiring swimmer who realizes he has already swum more than halfway across the lake but must now continue on to the other side before resting.

At this point the borderline must also deal with his separateness and recognize that he, not the therapist, has effected change. Like Dumbo, who first attributes his flying ability to his "magic feather" but then realizes it is due to his own talents, the borderline must begin to recognize and accept his own abilities to function independently. And he must develop new coping mechanisms to replace the ones that no longer work.

As the borderline improves, the intensity of the transference diminishes. The anger, impulsive behaviors, and mood changes—often directed at, or for the benefit of, the therapist—become less severe. Panicky dependency may gradually wither and be replaced by a growing self-confidence; anger erupts less often, replaced by greater determination to be in charge of one's own life. Impatience and caprice diminish, because the borderline begins to develop a separate sense of identity that can evolve without the need for attachment.

Countertransference

Countertransference refers to the therapist's own emotional reactions to the patient, which are based less on realistic considerations than on the therapist's past experiences and needs. An example is the doctor who perceives the patient as more needy and helpless than is truly the case because of the doctor's need to be a caretaker, to perceive himself as compassionate, and to avoid confrontation.

The borderline is often very perceptive about others, including the therapist. This sensitivity often provokes the therapist's own unresolved feelings. The doctor's needs for appreciation, affection, and control can sometimes prompt him into inappropriate behavior. He may be overly protective of the patient and encourage dependency. He may be overly controlling, demanding that the patient carry out his directions. He may complain of his own problems and induce the patient to take care of him. He may even enter into a sexual relationship with the patient "to teach intimacy." The therapist may rationalize all these as necessary for a "very sick" patient, but in reality they are satisfying his own needs.

The borderline can provoke feelings of anger, frustration, self-doubt, and a hopelessness in the therapist that mirrors his own. Goaded into emotions that challenge his professional self-worth, the therapist may experience genuine countertransference hate for the patient and view him as untreatable. Treatment of the borderline personality can be so infuriating that the term "borderline" has been inaccurately used sometimes by professionals as a derogatory label for any patient who is extremely irritating or who does not respond well to therapy. In these cases "borderline" more accurately reflects the countertransference frustration of a therapist than a scientific diagnosis of his patient.

THE PATIENT-THERAPIST "FIT"

All of the treatments described in this chapter can be productive approaches to the borderline patient. None have proved to be superior to the others. No therapeutic techniques have been shown to be uniformly curative in all cases. The only factor that seems to correlate consistently with improvement is a positive, mutually respectful relationship between patient and therapist.

Even when a doctor is successful in treating one or many borderline patients, this does not guarantee automatic success in treating others. The primary determining factor of success is usually a positive, optimistic feeling shared between the participants—a kind of patient-therapist "fit."

A good fit is difficult to define precisely, but refers to the abilities of both the patient and therapist to tolerate the predict-able turbulence of therapy, while maintaining a sturdy alliance while therapy takes place.

The Therapist's Role

Because treatment of BPD may entail a combination of several therapies—individual, group and family psychotherapies, medications, and hospitalization—the therapist's role in treat-ment may be as varied as the different therapies available. The doctor may be confrontational or non-directive; he may either spontaneously exhort and suggest, or initiate fewer interactions and expect the patient to assume a heavier burden for the pro-gress of psychotherapy. More important than the particular doctor or treatment method is the feeling of comfort and trust enjoyed by both patient and therapist. Both must sense commit-ment, reliability, and true partnership from the other.

To achieve this feeling of mutual comfort, both patient and doctor must understand and share common objectives. They should agree upon methods and have compatible styles. Most importantly, the therapist must recognize when he is treating a borderline patient.

The therapist should suspect that he is dealing with BPD when he takes on a patient whose past psychiatric history in-cludes contradictory diagnoses, multiple past hospitalizations, or trials of many medications. The patient may report being "kicked out" of previous therapies and becoming persona non grata in the local emergency room, having frequented the E.R. enough times to have earned a nickname (such as "Overdose Eddie") from the medical staff.

The experienced doctor will also be able to trust his countertransference reactions to the patient. Borderlines usually elicit very strong emotional reactions from others, including therapists. If early on in the evaluation, the therapist experiences strong feelings of wanting to protect or rescue the patient, of responsibility for the patient, or of extreme anger toward the patient, he should recognize that his intense responses may signal reactions to a borderline personality.

Choosing a Therapist

Therapists with differing styles may perform equally well with borderlines. Conversely, doctors who possess special expertise or interest in BPD and who generally do well with borderline patients cannot guarantee success with every patient.

A patient can choose from a variety of mental health professionals. Though psychiatrists have years of training in psychotherapy techniques (and, as physicians, are the only professionals capable of dealing with concurrent medical illnesses, prescribing medications, and arranging hospitalization), other skilled professionals—psychologists, social workers, counselors, psychiatric nurse-clinicians—may also attain expertise in psychotherapy with borderline patients.

In general, a therapist who works well with BPD possesses certain qualities that a prospective patient can usually recognize. He should be experienced in the treatment of BPD and remain tolerant and accepting in order to help the patient develop object constancy (see Chapter 2). He should be flexible and innovative, in order to adapt to the contortions through which therapy with a borderline may twist him. He should possess a sense of humor or at least a clear sense of proportion to present an appropriate model for the patient and to protect himself from the relentless intensity that such therapy requires.

Just as the doctor evaluates the patient during the initial assessment interviews, so should the patient evaluate the doctor to determine if they can work together profitably.

First, the patient should consider whether he is comfortable with the therapist's personality and style. Will he be able to talk with him openly and candidly? Is he too intimidating, too pushy, too wimpy, too seductive?

Secondly, do his assessment and goals coincide with the patient's? Treatment should be a collaboration in which both parties share the same view and use the same language. What should therapy hope to achieve? How will you know when you get there? About how long should it take?

Finally, are the recommended methods acceptable to the patient? There should be agreement on the type of psychotherapy advocated and the suggested frequency of meetings. Will the doctor and patient meet individually or together with others? Will there be a combination of approaches, which might include, say, individual therapy on a weekly basis, along with intermittent conjoint meetings with the spouse? Will therapy be more exploratory or more supportive? Will medications or hospitalization likely be employed? What kinds of medicines and which hospitals?

This initial assessment period usually requires at least one interview, often more. Both the patient and the doctor should be evaluating their ability and willingness to work with the other. Such an evaluation should be recognized as a kind of "no-fault" interchange: It is irrelevant and probably impossible to blame the therapist or the patient for the inability to establish rapport. It is necessary only to determine whether a therapeutic alliance is possible. However, if a patient continues to find every psychotherapist he sees unacceptable, his commitment to treatment should be questioned. He should consider the possibility that he is merely avoiding therapy, and should perhaps choose an admittedly imperfect doctor and get on with the task of getting better.

Obtaining a Second Opinion

Once therapy is underway, it is not unusual for treatment to stop and start, or for the form of therapy to change over time. Adjustments may be necessary because the borderline may require changes in his treatment as he progresses.

Sometimes, however, it is difficult to distinguish when therapy is stuck from when it is working through painful issues; it is sometimes difficult to separate dependency and fear of moving on from the agonizing realization of unfinished business. At such times there will arise a question of whether to proceed along the same lines or to take a step back and regroup. At this point a consultation with another doctor may be indicated.

Often the treating therapist will suggest this, but sometimes the patient must consider this option on his own.

Although the patient may fear that a doctor is offended by a request for consultation, a competent and secure therapist would not object or be defensive about such a request. It is, however, an area for exploration in the therapy, in order to assess whether the patient's wish for a second evaluation might constitute a running away from difficult issues or represent an unconscious angry rebuke. A second opinion may be helpful for both the patient and the doctor in providing a fresh outlook on the process of treatment.

Getting the Most from Therapy

Appreciating treatment as a collaborative alliance is the most important step in maximizing therapy. The borderline frequently loses sight of this primary principle. Instead, he sometimes approaches treatment as if the purpose were to please the doctor or to fight with him, to be taken care of or to pretend to have no problems.

The borderline may need to be frequently reminded of the parameters of therapy. He should understand the ground rules, including the doctor's availability and limitations, the time and resource constraints, and the agreed upon mutual goals.

The patient must not lose sight of the fact that he is bravely committing himself, his time, and his resources to the frightening task of trying to understand himself better and to effect alterations in his life patterns. Honesty in therapy is therefore of paramount importance for the *patient's* sake. He must not conceal painful areas or play games with the therapist to whom he has entrusted his care. He should abandon his need to control, or wish to be liked by, the therapist. In the borderline's quest to satisfy a presumed role, he may lose sight of the fact that it is not his obligation to please the therapist but to work with him as an equal.

Most important, the patient should always feel that he is actively collaborating in his treatment. He should avoid either the extreme of assuming a totally passive role, completely controlled by the doctor, or that of becoming a competitive, contentious rival, unwilling to listen to contributions from the therapist. Molding a viable relationship with the therapist becomes the borderline's first and, initially, most important task in embarking on a journey toward mental health.

INDIVIDUAL THERAPIES

Most clinicians divide individual therapy approaches into exploratory and supportive techniques. Though both styles overlap, they are distinguished by the intensity of therapy and the strategies utilized.

Exploratory Therapy

Exploratory psychotherapy, as recommended by Otto Kernberg, James Masterson and others for treatment of borderlines, is a modification of classical analysis. Sessions are usually conducted three or more times per week. This form of individual therapy is more intensive than supportive therapy, and has a more ambitious goal—to alter personality structure. The therapist provides little direct guidance to the patient, utilizing confrontation instead to point out the destructiveness of specific behaviors and to interpret unconscious behaviors in the hopes of eradicating them.

As in less intensive forms of therapy, a primary focus is on here-and-now issues. Genetic reconstruction, with its concentration on childhood and developmental issues, is important, but emphasized less than in classical psychoanalysis. The major goals in the early stages of treatment are to diminish behaviors that are self-destructive and disruptive to the treatment process (including prematurely terminating therapy), to solidify the patient's commitment to change, and to establish a trusting, reliable relationship between patient and doctor. Later stages emphasize the processes of formulating a separate, self-accepting sense of identity, establishing constant and trusting relationships, and tolerating aloneness and separations (including those from the therapist) adaptively.[2 3] Of course, these stages overlap.

Transference in exploratory therapy is more intense than in supportive therapy. Dependency on the therapist, together with idealization and devaluation, are experienced more passionately, as in classical psychoanalysis. Most therapists estimate the duration of treatment to be a minimum of four years, but often six to ten years.

Supportive Therapy

Supportive individual therapy, the most common form of therapy used for borderline personality, is usually conducted on a once weekly basis. Direct advice, education, and reassurance replace the confrontation and interpretation of unconscious material typically used in exploratory therapy.

This approach is meant to be less intense and to bolster more adaptive defenses. In supportive psychotherapy the doctor may reinforce suppression, discouraging discussion of painful memories that cannot be resolved. Rather than question the roots of minor obsessive concerns, the therapist may encourage them as "hobbies" or minor eccentricities. For example, a patient's need to keep his apartment spotless may not be dissected as to causes, but be acknowledged as a useful means to retain a sense of mastery and control when feeling overwhelmed. This contrasts with psychoanalysis, in which the aim is to analyze defenses and then eradicate them.

Focusing on current, more practical issues, supportive therapy tries to quash suicidal and other self-destructive behaviors rather than to explore them fully. Impulsive actions and chaotic interpersonal relationships are identified and confronted, without necessarily acquiring insight into the underlying factors that caused them.

Supportive therapy most often continues on a once weekly frequency for four to five years before proceeding on an as-needed basis. Intermittent contacts may continue indefinitely and the therapist's continued availability may be very important. Therapy gradually terminates when other lasting relationships form, and when outside, gratifying activities become more important in the patient's life.

In supportive therapy the patient tends to be less dependent on the therapist and to form a less intense transference. Though some clinicians argue that this form of therapy is less likely to institute lasting change in borderline patients, others have induced significant behavioral modifications in borderline patients with this kind of treatment.[4]

Dr. Ralph Greenson used a combination of supportive and

exploratory therapies in his treatment of Marilyn Monroe. Though supportive therapy had only recently come into vogue in the late fifties (and the borderline diagnosis was more than twenty years from being formally adopted), he sensed Marilyn's need for something more consoling and structured than classical psychoanalysis.

He allowed Marilyn to become friendly with his family, even to the extent of having her as a guest in his home. He told Norman Rosten that she needed both supportive and analytical psychotherapy because "the treatment has to suit the patient." In her case, he felt she needed actual experiences in her present life to compensate for the emotional deprivation of her childhood.[5]

Interestingly, Freud's examination office was in his home and he often allowed contacts between his patients and his family. But Greenson realized that allowing Marilyn to form attachments to his family was considered professionally inappropriate, though he felt it necessary for effective treatment.

> It may seem to you that I have broken rules, but I feel that if I am fortunate enough, perhaps some years from now, Marilyn may become a psychoanalytic patient. She is not ready for it now. I feel I can tell you these things because she considers you and Hedda her closest friends and there must be somebody with whom I can share my responsibilities. By the way, I have spoken to Marilyn and she has given me permission to talk to you in general terms about herself.[6]

GROUP THERAPIES

Treating the borderline in a group makes perfect sense. A group allows the borderline patient to dilute the intensity of feelings directed toward one individual (such as the therapist) by recognizing emotions stimulated by others. In a group the borderline can more easily control the constant struggle between emotional closeness and distance; unlike individual therapy, in which the spotlight is always on him, the borderline can attract or avoid attention in a group. Confrontations by other group members may sometimes be more readily accepted than those from the idealized or devalued therapist, because a peer may be perceived as someone "who really knows what I'm going through."

The borderline's demandingness, egocentrism, isolating withdrawal, abrasiveness and social deviance can all be more effectively challenged by group peers. In addition, the borderline may accept more readily the group's expressions of hope, caring and altruism.[7,8,9]

The progress of other group members serves as a model for growth. When a group patient attains a goal, he serves as an inspiration to others in the group who have observed his growth and have vicariously shared his successes. The rivalry and competition so characteristic of borderline relationships are vividly demonstrated within the group setting and can be identified and addressed in ways that would be inaccessible in individual therapy. Finally, a group provides a living, breathing experimental laboratory in which the borderline can attempt different patterns of behavior with other people, without the risk of penalties from the "outside world."

Because of the demands on the borderline patient in group therapy, most therapists recommend combining group with individual treatment, so as to maintain individualized support for the patient. Therapists disagree, however, on the ideal composition of the groups. Some feel that groups composed exclusively of borderlines are most effective because they allow maximum identification with others experiencing similar struggles. But most believe that borderlines fare better in a mixed group, consisting of other borderline patients and healthier patients who serve as models for more adaptive ways of functioning. Non-borderline patients also benefit from this mix, for they may have difficulty accessing their own emotions. The borderline can stimulate feelings and serve as a model for expressing emotions.[10]

Yet, research on group therapy as a treatment for BPD is surprisingly spare. The very features that make group therapy a potentially attractive treatment for borderlines are the very reasons many such patients resist group settings. The demand for individual attention, envy and distrust of others, the contradictory wish for, and fear of, intense closeness, all contribute to the reluctance of many borderline patients to enter group treatment. Higher functioning borderlines can tolerate these frustrations of group therapy and use the "in vivo" experiences to address defects in interrelating. Lower-functioning borderlines, however, often won't join and, if they do, won't stay.

The borderline patient may experience significant obstacles in group therapy. His self-absorption and lack of empathy often prevent involvement with others' problems. If the borderline's concerns are too deviant or the material too intense, he may feel isolated and disconnected. For example, a patient who discusses childhood incest, or deviant sexual practices, or severe chemical abuse may fear that he may shock the other group members. And, indeed, some members may have difficulty relating to upsetting material. When several borderlines are in a group, they may share the feeling that their needs are not being met by the therapist. In such situations they may attempt to take care of each other in ways they wished they were being cared for. This may lead to contacts between patients outside of the group setting and perpetuation of dependency needs as they try to "treat" each other. Romances or even business dealings between group members usually end disastrously, because these patients will not be able to use the group objectively to explore the relationship, which is often a continuation of unproductive searches to be cared for.

Elaine, a twenty-nine-year-old woman, was referred for group therapy after two years of individual psychotherapy. The oldest of four daughters, Elaine was sexually abused by her father, starting around age five and continuing for over ten years. She perceived her mother as weak and ineffectual and her father as demanding and unable to be pleased. In adolescence, she became the caretaker for the whole family. As her sisters married and had children, Elaine remained single, entering college and then graduate school. She had few girlfriends and dated infrequently. Her only romantic relationships involved two married men, much older than she, who supervised her work. Most of her off-work time was devoted to organizing family functions, caring for ill family members, and generally taking care of family problems.

Isolated and depressed, Elaine sought individual therapy. Recognizing the limitations in her social functioning, she later requested a referral for group therapy. There, she quickly established a position as the helper for the others, denying any problems of her own. She often became angry with the therapist, whom she perceived as not helpful enough to the group members.

The group members encouraged Elaine to examine issues she had previously been unable to confront—her constant scowling and intimidating facial expressions and her subtly angry verbal exchanges. Although this process took many frustrating months, she was eventually able to acknowledge her disdain for women, which became obvious in the group setting. Elaine realized that her anger at the male therapist was actually transferred anger from her father and recognized her compulsive attempts to repeat this father-daughter relationship with other men. Elaine began to experiment in the group with new ways of interacting with men and women. Simultaneously, she was able to pull back from the suffocating immersion in her family's problems.

FAMILY THERAPIES

Family therapy is a very logical approach to the treatment of the borderline patient, who often emerges from disturbed relationships with parents engaged in persistent conflicts that may eventually entangle the borderline's own spouse and children.

Though family therapy is sometimes implemented with outpatients, it is most often invoked as part of in-hospital treatment, where individual and other supportive therapies can be simultaneously administered. In addition, the family's resistance to participating in treatment can be more easily overcome following a crisis situation that necessitated the hospitalization.

The families of borderlines often balk at treatment for several reasons. They may feel guilt over the patient's problems and fear being blamed for them. Also the bonds in borderline family systems are often very strong; family members are often suspicious of outsiders and fearful of change. Though family members may be colluding in the perpetuation of the patient's behaviors (consciously or unconsciously), the attitude of the family is often, "Make him better, but don't blame us and, most of all, don't change us."[11]

Yet it is imperative to gain some support from the family, for without it therapy may be sabotaged. For adolescents and young adults, family therapy involves the patient and his parents, and sometimes his siblings. For the adult borderline who is married or involved seriously in a romantic relationship, family therapy will often include the spouse or lover and sometimes the couple's children.

The dynamics of borderline family interaction usually adopt one of two extremes—either very strongly entangled or very detached. In the former case, it is important to build an alliance with all family members, for without their support, the patient may not be able to maintain treatment independently. When the family is estranged, the therapist must carefully assess the potential impact of family involvement: If reconciliation is possible and healthy, it may be an important goal; if, however, it appears that reconciliation may be detrimental or hopelessly unrealistic, the patient may need to relinquish fantasies of reunion. In fact, mourning the loss of an idealized family interrelationship may become a major milestone in therapy.

Debbie, a twenty-six-year-old woman, entered the hospital with a history of depression, self-mutilation, alcoholism, and bulimia. Family assessment meetings revealed an ambivalent, but basically supportive relationship with her husband. The course of therapy began to focus on previously undisclosed episodes of sexual abuse by an older neighbor boy, starting when the patient was about eight years old. In addition to sexually abusing her, this boy had also forced her to share liquor with him and then would make her drink his urine from the bottle, which she would later vomit. He had also cut her when she tried to refuse his advances.

These past incidents were re-enacted in her current pathology. As these memories unfolded, Debbie became more conscious of longstanding rage at her alcoholic, passive father and at her weak, disinterested mother, whom she perceived as unable to protect her. Although she had previously maintained a distant, superficial relationship with her parents, she now requested an opportunity to meet with them in family therapy to reveal her past hurts and disappointment in them.

As she predicted, her parents were very uncomfortable with these revelations. But for the first time Debbie was able to confront her father's alcoholism and her disappointment in him and in her mother's detachment. At the same time all could confirm their love for each other and acknowledge the difficulties in expressing it. Although she recognized there would be no significant changes in their relationship, Debbie felt she had accomplished much and was more comfortable in accepting the distance and failures in the family interactions.

Therapeutic approaches to family therapy are similar to those for individual treatment. A thorough history is important and may include the construction of a family tree. Such a diagram may stimulate exploration of how grandparents, godparents, namesakes, or other important relatives may influence family interactions across generations.

As in individual therapy, family therapy approaches may be primarily supportive-educational or exploratory-reconstructive. In the former, the therapist's primary goals are to ally with the family; minimize conflicts, guilt, and defensiveness; and unite them in working toward mutually supportive objectives. Exploratory-reconstructive family therapy is more ambitious, directed more toward recognizing the members' complementary roles within the family system and attempting actively to change these roles.

At one point in therapy, Elaine focused on her relationship with her parents. After confronting them with the revelation of her father's sexual abuse, she continued to feel frustrated with them. Both parents refused further discussion about the abuse and discouraged her from continuing in therapy. Elaine was puzzled by their behavior—sometimes they were very dependent and clinging; other times she felt infantilized, especially when they insistently continued to refer to her by her childhood nickname. Elaine requested family meetings, to which they reluctantly agreed.

During these meetings Elaine's father gradually admitted that her accusations were true, though he continued to deny any recollection of his assaults. Her mother realized that in many ways she had been emotionally unavailable to her husband and children and recognized her own indirect responsibility for the abuse. Elaine learned for the first time that her father had also been sexually abused during his childhood. The therapy succeeded in releasing skeletons from the closet and establishing better communication in the family. Elaine and her parents began for the first time speaking to each other as adults.

EXPRESSIVE THERAPIES

Individual, group, and family therapies require patients to express their thoughts and feelings with words, but the borderline patient is often somewhat handicapped in this area, more likely to exhibit inner concerns through actions rather than words. Expressive therapies utilize art, music, literature, physical movement, and drama to encourage communication in nonverbal ways.

In art therapy, patients are encouraged to create drawings, paintings, collages, self-portraits, clay sculpture, dolls and so on that express inner feelings. In our Comprehensive Treatment Unit (CTU) at Saint John's Mercy Medical Center in St. Louis, patients are presented with a book of blank pages, in which they are invited to draw representations of a variety of experiences, such as inner secrets, closeness, or hidden fears.

Music therapy uses melodies and lyrics to stimulate feelings that may otherwise be inaccessible. Music often unlocks emotions and promotes meditation in a calm environment.

Body movement and dance use physical exertion to express emotions. In another type of expressive therapy called psychodrama, patients and the "therapist-director" act out specific problems of the patient. Bibliotherapy is another therapy technique in which patients read and discuss literature, short stories, plays, poetry, movies, and videos. Edward Albee's *Who's Afraid of Virginia Woolf?* is a popular play to read, and, especially perform, because its emotional scenes provide a catharsis as patients recite lines of rage and disappointment that reflect problems in their own lives.

Irene's chronic depression was related to sexual abuses that she had endured at an early age from her older brother and that she had only recently begun to remember. At 25 and living alone, she was flooded with recollections of these early encounters and eventually required hospitalization as her depression worsened. Because she felt overwhelmed by guilt and self-blame, she was unable to verbalize her memories to others, or allow herself to experience the underlying anger.

During an expressive-therapy program that combined art and music, the therapists worked with Irene to help her become more aware of the fury that she was avoiding. She was encouraged to draw what her anger felt like while loud, pulsating rock music played in the background. Astonishing herself, she drew penises, to which she then added mutilated disfigurements. Initially fearful and embarrased about these drawings, they soon made her aware and more accepting of her rage and obvious wish for retaliation.

As she discussed her emotional reactions to the drawings, she began to describe her past abuse and the accompanying feelings. Eventually, she began to talk more openly, individually with doctors, and in groups, which afforded her the opportunity to develop mastery over these frightening experiences, and to place them in proper perspective.

PHARMACOTHERAPY

The efficacy of medications for treating borderline patients remains unclear. Because the borderline syndrome borders so closely on other illnesses—such as schizophrenia and depression—drugs useful for these other conditions have been tried with borderline patients. Most authorities agree that medications are more likely to be effective when specific symptoms, such as psychosis or classical depression, are overt rather than masked, and when there is a clear family history of these maladies or response to these drugs among blood relatives.

Although drugs may relieve some significantly debilitating symptoms, they are not expected to alter longstanding personality characteristics or behavior patterns. Further, pharmacotherapy must be used judiciously since borderline patients easily develop physiological or psychological drug dependencies. Of the classes of medications outlined in Appendix C, only the minor tranquilizers present a significant potential hazard of physical addiction.

One significant complication in treating borderline patients is their tendency to "split"—not only people but also treatment approaches (see Chapter 2). Some borderlines idealize psychotherapeutic approaches as the only legitimate way to improve, and denigrate pharmacotherapy as a kind of mind control designed to chemically straitjacket them into submission. Other borderlines accept medication as the only scientific approach to curing their "chemical imbalance," and devalue psychotherapy, used by the therapist to promote dependency as a process for financial gain. When combined treatment is indicated (as is often necessary), the psychiatrist must carefully present to the patient the rationales for each approach.[12][13][14][15]

For detailed discussion of medications used in treating BPD, see Appendix C.

HOSPITALIZATION

Borderline patients constitute a significant proportion of all hospitalized psychiatric patients, and BPD is far and away the most common personality disorder encountered in the hospital setting.[16] The borderline's propensities for impulsivity, self-destructive behaviors (suicide, drug overdoses), and brief psychotic episodes are the usual acute precipitants of hospitalization.

The hospital provides a structured milieu to help contain and organize the borderline's chaotic world. The support and involvement of other patients and staff present the borderline with important feedback that challenges some of his perceptions and validates others.

The hospital minimizes the borderline's conflicts in the external world and provides greater opportunity for intensive self-examination. It also allows a respite from the intense relationship between the borderline and his outpatient therapist and permits diffusion of this intensity onto other staff members within the hospital setting. In this more neutral milieu, the patient can reevaluate his personal goals and program of therapy.

At first, the inpatient borderline typically protests admission, but by the time of discharge he is fully ensconced in the hospital setting, often fearful of discharge. He has an urgent need to be cared for, yet at the same time may become a leader of the ward, trying to control and "help" other patients. At times he appears overwhelmed by his catastrophic problems; on other occasions he displays great creativity and initiative.

Characteristically, the hospitalized borderline creates a fascinating pas de deux of splitting and projective identification (see Chapter 2) with staff members. Some staff perceive the borderline as a pathetic, but appealing gamin; others see him as a calculating, sadistic manipulator. These disparate views emerge when the patient splits staff members into all good (supportive, understanding) and all bad (confrontive, demanding) projections, much like he does with other people in his life. When staff members accept the assigned projections—both "good" ("You're the only one who understands me") and "bad" ("You don't really care; you're only in it for the paycheck")— the projective identification circle is completed: Conflict erupts between the "good" staff and the "bad" staff.

Amidst this struggle the hospitalized borderline recapitulates his external world interpersonal patterns: a seductive wish for protection, which ultimately leads to disappointment, then to feelings of abandonment, finally to self-destructive behaviors and emotional retreat.

Therapeutic approaches to the hospitalized borderline patient are distinguished primarily by the time period proposed for confinement. Although there are no clear-cut demarcations, short-term hospitalization generally extends for several weeks, but usually less than three months. Long-term hospitalization is usually at least six months but may extend as long as two to three years, and sometimes longer. All of the therapies discussed above may be integral parts of hospital care.[17]

Short-term Hospitalization

Due to increasing hospital costs and declining insurance coverage, short-term hospitalization is more common for most psychiatric patients. However, some psychiatrists feel that brief hospitalization is preferable for all borderline patients regardless of expense or inconvenience because it minimizes opportunities for regression and avoids the development of extreme dependency, both of which occur during longer confinements.

Inpatient care usually follows crises, such as suicide attempts, violent outbursts, psychotic breaks, self-destructive episodes (chemical abuse, anorexia/bulimia, or gambling). Hospitalization is also indicated for diagnostic evaluation and consultation for the outpatient therapist when progress in therapy is stalled.[18] Short-term hospitalization may also be necessary as a preventative measure, in anticipation of impending crises. For example, a borderline patient who is overly dependent on her dying mother may benefit from a short hospital confinement in order to prepare for working through her grief and to short-circuit an anticipated suicide gesture. Fragile patients who have been maintained outside the hospital may benefit from a short hospitalization when predictable external events (especially separations), such as the finalization of a divorce, or an extended therapist's vacation, loom threateningly and anticipate disruption of an uneasy calm.

The hospital milieu focuses on structure and limit-setting. Support and positive rapport are emphasized. Treatment centers around practical, adaptive responses to turmoil. Vocational and daily living skills are evaluated. Conjoint meetings with family, when appropriate, are initiated. A formalized contract between patient and staff may help solidify mutual expectations and limits. Such a contract may outline the daily therapy program, which the patient is obligated to attend, and the patient's specific goals for the hospitalization, which the staff agrees to address with him.

The primary goals of short-term hospitalization include resolving the precipitating crises, terminating destructive behaviors, and relieving severe depression and anxiety. Personal and environmental strengths are identified and bolstered. Important therapy issues are uncovered or reevaluated and modifications for outpatient therapy may be recommended. Deeper exploration of these issues is limited on a short-term, inpatient unit, and is more thoroughly pursued on an outpatient basis or during long-term hospitalization. Since the overriding concern is to return the patient to the outside world as quickly as possible, plans for discharge and after care commence immediately upon admission.[19]

Long-Term Hospitalization

Today, extensive hospitalization is reserved for the very wealthy or for those with exceptional insurance coverage for psychiatric illness. Proponents of long-term hospitalization recognize the dangers of regression but argue that true personality change requires extensive and intensive treatment. Indications for long-term confinement include chronically low motivation, inadequate or harmful social supports (such as enmeshment in a pathological family system), severe impairments in functioning which preclude holding a job or being self-sufficient, and repeated failures at outpatient therapy and short hospitalizations. Such features make early return to the outside environment unlikely.

During longer hospitalizations, the milieu may be less highly structured. The patient is encouraged to assume more shared responsibility for treatment. In addition to current, practical concerns, the staff and patient explore past, archetypal patterns of behavior and transference issues. The hospital can function like a laboratory, in which the borderline identifies specific problems and experiments with solutions in his interactions with staff and other patients.

Eventually, Jennifer (see Chapter 1) entered a long-term hospital. She spent the first six months in the closet—literally and figuratively. She would often sit in her bedroom closet, hiding from the staff. After a while she became more involved with her therapist, getting angry at him and attempting to provoke his rage. She alternately demanded and begged to leave. As the staff held firm, she talked more about her father, how he was like her husband, how he was like all men. Jennifer began to share her feelings with the female staff, something that had always been difficult because of her distrust of and disrespect for women. Later during the hospitalization, she decided to divorce her husband and give up custody of her son. Although these actions hurt her, she considered them "unselfish selfishness"—trying to take care of herself was the most self-sacrificing and caring thing she could do for those she loved. She eventually returned to school and sought a professional degree.

The goals of longer hospitalization extend those of short-term care—not only to identify dysfunctional areas, but also to modify these characteristics. Increased control of impulses, greater ability to trust and relate to others, a more defined sense of identity, and better tolerance of frustration are the clearest signs of a successful hospital treatment. Educational and vocational objectives may be achieved during an extensive hospitalization. Changes in unhealthy living arrangements—moving out of the home, divorce, etc.—may be completed.

The greatest potential hazard of long-term hospitalization is regression. If staff do not actively confront and motivate the patient, the borderline can become mired in an even more helpless position, in which he is even more dependent on others to direct his life.[20]

Partial Hospitalization

Partial (or day) hospital care is a form of therapy in which the patient attends hospital activities during the day and then returns home in the evening. Other partial hospital programs may be held in the evenings, following work or school, and may allow sleeping accommodations when alternatives are not available.

This innovative approach allows the borderline to benefit from the intensity and structure of hospital care, while maintaining an independent living situation. Hospital dependency occurs less frequently. Because partial hospitalization is usually much less expensive than traditional inpatient care, it may be favored for cost considerations.

Borderlines who require more intensive care, but not twenty-four-hour supervision, who are in danger of severe regression if hospitalized, who are making a transition out of the hospital to the outside world, who must maintain vocational or academic pursuits while requiring hospital care, who experience severe financial limitations on care, may all benefit from this treatment. The hospital milieu and therapy objectives are similar to those of the associated inpatient program.[21, 22]

Most of the studies on the effectiveness of hospitalization for borderline patients focus on long-term facilities. These findings primarily demonstrate significant improvement in patients after discharge. One study found that the most significant predictor of positive outcome to hospitalization was a valued patient-therapist relationship.[23] More studies are needed to monitor the effects of short-term care. Comparative studies are also required to evaluate the effectiveness of various types of hospital programs, including the advantages and disadvantages of inpatient units composed exclusively of borderline patients.

CAN BORDERLINES BE CURED?

Since no specific therapy seems superior to the others, the choice of treatment is most often dictated by nontherapeutic considerations, such as time and financial resources, therapist availability, and so on. Even more important is the question of whether therapy helps at all. Some studies estimate that as many as 50 percent of borderline patients drop out of treatment within six months; only approximately one out of ten patients complete the course of therapy, which usually extends for several years.[24]

Some have argued that borderlines eventually "mature out" of their pathology spontaneously and that therapy does not substantially affect this natural process. "Fortunately, psychoanalysis is not the only way to resolve inner conflicts," wrote Karen Horney in *Our Inner Conflicts*. "Life itself remains a very effective therapist." However, recent studies imply a significant suicide rate among borderlines (8 to 10 percent).[5] So first, they have to stay alive long enough to get better.

Studies attempting to track the progress of borderline patients, with and without treatment, generally agree that treatment is significantly beneficial. Most of these studies have examined individual therapy, both in and out of the hospital. Appropriate drug treatment successfully relieves many serious symptoms. Psychotherapy also clearly produces improvement. Although most patients continue to have some difficulty with routine functioning and may continue to exhibit remnants of ingrained characterological patterns, and therefore may not be considered completely "cured," they often no longer satisfy the criteria that define the diagnosis of BPD.[1,26]

Such patients also display a greater capacity to trust and establish satisfactory (even if not very close) relationships. They have a clearer sense of direction and a more stable sense of themselves. In a sense, then, they have become better borderlines.

"You always spoke of unconditional acceptance," said one borderline patient to her therapist, "and somewhere in the recent past I finally began to feel it. It's wonderful . . . . You gave me a safe place to unravel—to unfold. I was lost somewhere inside my mind. You gave me enough acceptance and freedom to finally let my true self out."

8

Coping with the Borderline

"But he's a human being, and a terrible thing is happening to him. So attention must be paid. He is not to be allowed to fall into his grave like an old dog. Attention must be finally paid to such a person."
—From Death of a Salesman by Arthur Miller

NO ONE KNEW quite what to do with Ray. He had been in and out of hospitals and had seen many doctors over the years, but he could never remain long in treatment. Nor could he stay with a job. His wife, Denise, worked in a dentist's office and spent most of her leisure time with her friends, generally ignoring Ray's complaints of chest pains, headaches, backaches, and depression.

Ray was the only child of wealthy, protective parents. When he was nine, his father's brother committed suicide. Although he never knew his uncle very well, he understood that his parents were greatly affected by the suicide. After this event, his parents became even more protective and would insist he stay home from school whenever he felt ill. At the age of twelve, Ray announced he was depressed and began seeing what became a parade of therapists.

An indifferent student, he went on to college where he met Denise. She was the only woman who had ever shown any interest in him, and after a short courtship they were married. Both quit college and dutifully went to work, but relied on Ray's parents to subsidize their household and Ray's continuing therapy.

The couple moved frequently; whenever Denise got bored with a job or a location, they would move to a different part of the country. She would quickly acquire a new job and new friends, but Ray had great difficulty and would remain out of work for many months.

As they both began drinking more, their fighting worsened. When they battled, Ray would sometimes leave and return to live with his parents; there he would stay until the family began to quarrel and then he'd return to Denise.

Frequently Ray's wife and parents would get fed up with his moodiness and multiple medical complaints, but then he'd threaten to kill himself and his parents would become panic-stricken. They insisted he see new doctors and flew him around the country to consult with various experts. They arranged hospitalizations in several prestigious institutions, but after a short time Ray always signed himself out against medical advice, and his parents would send him plane fare home. They continuously vowed to withhold further financial support but never stuck to their word.

Friends and jobs became an indistinguishable blur of un-satisfying encounters. Whenever new acquaintance or occupation disappointed in any way, Ray quit. His parents wrung their hands; Denise basically ignored him. Ray continued spinning out of control with no one to limit him, including himself.

RECOGNIZING BPD IN FRIENDS AND RELATIONS

On the surface a borderline personality can be very difficult to identify, despite the underlying volcanic turbulence. Unlike many people afflicted with other mental disorders—such as schizophrenia, bipolar (manic-depressive) disease, alcoholism, or eating disorders—the borderline can usually function ex-tremely well in work and social situations without appearing overtly pathological. Indeed, some of the hallmarks of border-line behavior are the sudden, unpredictable eruptions of anger, extreme suspiciousness, or suicidal depression from someone who has appeared so "normal."

The borderline's sudden outbursts are usually very frighten-ing and mystifying—both to the borderline himself and to those closest to him. Because of the sudden and extreme nature of certain prominent symptoms, the concerned party can be easily misled and not recognize that it is a manifestation of BPD rather than a separate primary illness. For example, a person who attempts to kill himself by overdosing or cutting his wrists may be diagnosed with depression, and prescribed antidepressant medications and brief, supportive psychotherapy. If the patient is suffering from a chemical depression, this regimen should improve his condition and he should recover relatively quickly and completely. If, however, the destructive behaviors have been triggered by BPD, his self-harming will continue, unabated by the treatment. Even if he is both depressed and borderline (a common combination), this approach will only partially treat the illness and further problems will ensue. If the borderline fea-tures are not recognized, the continuation of suicidal or other destructive behaviors, despite treatment, becomes puzzling and frustrating for the patient, the doctor, and everyone concerned.

Abby, a twenty-three-year-old fashion model, was treated in a chemical dependency unit for alcoholism. She responded very well to this program, but as she continued to abstain from alcohol, she became increasingly, compulsively bulimic. She then entered an eating-disorders unit in which she was again successfully treated.

A few weeks later, she began experiencing severe panic epi-sodes in stores, offices, even while driving in her car, and eventually became afraid to leave her house. In addition to these phobias, she was becoming more depressed. As she considered entrance to a phobia clinic, a psychiatric consultant recognized all of her symptoms to be representative of BPD and recom-mended instead admission to a psychiatric unit specializing in borderline conditions. Where her previous treatments had fo-cused exclusively on alcoholism or bulimia, this hospitalization took a more holistic view of her life.

Eventually, Abby was able to connect her problems to her continued ambivalent relationship with her parents, who had interfered with her attempts to separate, mature, and be more independent. She realized that her various illnesses were really means to escape her parents' demands without guilt. Her bulimia, drinking, and anxieties occupied all her energy, distracting her from addressing the conflicts with her parents. Further, her "sick" role excused her from even feeling obligated to work on this relationship. The illnesses also kept her attached to them: Because her parents had serious marital problems (her mother was an alcoholic and her father was chronically depressed), she could stay close to them by replicating their roles.

After a brief hospitalization she continued individual outpatient psychotherapy. Her mood improved and her anxieties and phobias dissolved to a great degree. She also continued to abstain from alcohol and purging.

Abby's case illustrates how a prominent behavior may actually represent an underlying BPD in which one or more of its features—unstable relationships, impulsivity, mood shifts, intense anger, suicidal threats, identity disturbances, feelings of emptiness, or frantic efforts to avoid abandonment—result in psychiatric symptoms that might mistakenly lead to incomplete diagnosis or even misdiagnosis.

COPING AND HELPING

It is important to remember that BPD is an illness, not a willful attempt to get attention. The borderline lacks the boots, much less the bootstraps, with which to pull himself up. It is useless to get angry or to cajole and plead with the borderline to change; without help he is bereft of the tools to alter his behavior.

However, this does not imply that the borderline is helpless and should not be held responsible for his behavior. Actually, the opposite is true. He must accept, without being excused or protected, the real consequences of his actions, even though initially he may be powerless to alter them.

The borderline's extremes of behavior typically lead to either a hard-nosed "You lazy good-for-nothing SOB, pull yourself together and fly right" response, or a cajoling "You poor baby, you can't do it; I'll take care of you" pat on the head. All must be aware of how their interactions may encourage or inhibit borderline behaviors

Those who interact with a borderline must attempt to walk a

very thin line between, on the one hand, providing reassurance of the borderline's worthiness and, on the other, confirming the necessary expectations. They must try to respond supportively, but without overreacting. Affection and physical touching, such as hugging and holding a hand, can communicate to the borderline that he is a valued person, but if it is exploitative, it will hinder trust. If caring results in overprotectiveness, the borderline stops feeling responsible for his behavior.

In most settings, concentrating on the Truth segments of SET principles (see Chapter 6) can allow for reasonable guidelines. But when suicide is threatened, it is usually time to contact a mental health professional or suicide-prevention facility. Suicide threats should not be allowed to become "emotional blackmail," whereby the friend or relation is manipulated to behave as the borderline demands. Threats should be taken seriously and met with prompt, predictable, realistic reactions, such as demanding that the borderline obtain professional help (a Truth response).

Jack, a forty-one-year-old single man, worked part time while attempting to return to school. His widowed mother continued to support him financially, and whenever he failed at work, school, or with a relationship, she would reinforce his helplessness, by insisting he could not succeed in achieving his goals and suggesting he return "home" to live with her. Therapy involved not only helping Jack understand his wish to remain helpless and reap the inherent benefits of helplessness, but also confronted his mother's role in perpetuating his dependency.

It takes only one actor in the drama to initiate change. Jack's mother can respond to his dependency with SET responses that express her caring (Support), understanding (Empathy), and acknowledgment of reality (Truth)—the need for Jack to take responsibility for his own actions. If his mother is unwilling to alter her behavior, Jack must recognize her role in his problems and distance himself from her.

Contending with Borderline Rage

After awhile, for someone close to a borderline, unpredictable behaviors may become commonplace and therefore "predictably unpredictable." One of the most common, the angry outburst, usually comes with no warning and appears way out of proportion.

The close friend, relation, or coworker should resist the temptation to "fight fire with fire." The louder and angrier the borderline gets, the quieter and more composed the other person should become, thereby refusing to collaborate in aggravating the emotional atmosphere, and demonstrating the comparative outlandish intensity of the borderline's rage. If the concerned individual senses the potential for physical violence, he should leave the scene immediately. Borderline rage often cannot be reasoned with, so discussion and debate are unnecessary and may only worsen the situation. Instead, one should try to cool off the conflict by acknowledging the difference in opinion and agreeing to disagree. Further discussion can come later when the atmosphere is more settled.

Living with Borderline Mood Swings

Rapid mood changes can be equally perplexing to the borderline and to those around him. From an early age, Meredith had always been aware of her moodiness. Without reason she could soar to great heights of excitement and joy, only to plummet, without warning, to the lower reaches of despair. Her parents indulged her moodiness by tiptoeing softly around her, never challenging her irritability. In school, friends would come and go, put off by her unpredictability. Some called her "the manic-depressive" and tried to kid her out of her surliness.

Her husband, Ben, said he was attracted to her "kindness" and "sense of fun." But Meredith could change dramatically from playful to suicidal. Similarly, her interactions with Ben would change from joyful sharing to gloomy isolation. Her moods were totally unpredictable and Ben was never sure how he would find her upon his return at the end of the day. At times he felt that he should enter their home by putting his hat on a stick and poking it into the doorway to see if it would be embraced, ignored, or shot at.

Ben was locked into a typical borderline "Damned if you do and damned if you don't" scenario. Confronting her depression would prompt more withdrawal and anger, but ignoring it would seem to demonstrate lack of concern. The SET principles would address this conflict and insist on Meredith's input into how he (and others) should react to her moods.

For Meredith, these shifts in mood, unresponsive to a variety of medications, were equally distressing. Her task was to recognize such swings, take responsibility for having them, and learn to adapt by compensating for their presence. When in a state of depression, she could subsequently identify it and learn to explain to others around her that she was in a down phase and would try to function as well as she could. If she was with people to whom she could not comfortably explain her situation, Meredith could maintain a low profile and actively try to avoid dealing with some of the demands on her. A major goal would involve establishing constancy—consistent, reliable attitudes and behaviors—toward herself and others.

Handling Impulsivity

Impulsive acts can be extremely frustrating for the borderline's friends and relations, particularly if the acts are self-destructive. This trait is especially unnerving when it emerges (as it often does) at a relatively stable point in the borderline's life. Indeed, impulsive behaviors may emanate precisely because life is settling and the borderline feels uncomfortable in a crisis-free state.

Larry, for example, was in a marriage that was comfortably boring. Married for over twenty years, he and Phyllis rarely interacted. She reared their sons while Larry toiled for a large company. His life was a self-imposed prison of daily routine and compulsive behaviors. He took hours to dress, in order to arrange his clothing just so. At night before bed, he engaged in rituals to maintain a sense of control—the closet doors had to be opened in a special way, the bathroom sink had to be carefully cleaned, and the soap and toilet articles arranged in a certain pattern.

But within this tightly regimented routine, Larry would impulsively get drunk, pick fights, or abruptly leave town for an entire day without warning. On two occasions he impulsively overdosed on his heart medicine "to see what it felt like." Usually he would absorb Phyllis' anger by turning somber and quiet; but every so often he would strike out at her, often over trivial matters.

He would remain dry for several months and then, just as he was receiving praise for abstaining, he would get abusively and loudly drunk. His wife, friends, and counselors pleaded and threatened, but to no avail.

SET techniques might have helped Phyllis to deal with Larry's impulsivity. Rather than beg and threaten, she might have emphasized her caring for Larry and her growing realization that he was becoming more and more dissatisfied with his life. Truth statements would communicate her own unhappiness with their current situation and the crucial need to do something about it, such as enter therapy.

It is also often helpful to be able to predict impulsive behaviors from past experiences. For example, after a period of sobriety, Phyllis might remind Larry that in the past, when things have gone well, he has built up pressures that have exploded into drinking binges. By pointing out previous patterns, one can help the borderline become more aware of feelings that preview the onset of impulsivity. In addition, the borderline learns that behaviors that he has perceived as chaotic and unpredictable can actually be anticipated, understood, and thereby controlled.

Finally, in therapy, Larry began to see that his seemingly unpredictable behaviors represented anger at himself and others. He realized how he would become abusive to his wife or begin drinking when frustrated with himself. This impulsive behavior would result in guilt and self-chastisement, which, in turn, served to expiate his sins. As Larry began to value himself more highly and respect his own ideals and beliefs, his destructive activities diminished.

UNDERSTANDING YOUR OWN EMOTIONS

When you join the borderline on his roller-coaster ride, you also must expect to experience a variety of emotions, especially guilt, fear, and anger. When self-destructive, the borderline may appear helpless and project responsibility for his behavior onto others, who may all too readily accept it. Guilt, is a strong inhibitor of honest confrontation. Similarly, fear of physical harm—to the borderline, others or yourself—may also be a powerful deterrent to open interactions. Anger is a common reaction when, as frequently occurs, you feel manipulated or simply don't like or understand a certain behavior.

Lois' mother called Lois frequently, complaining of severe headaches, loneliness, and an overall disgust with life. With her father long dead and her siblings estranged from the family, Lois was the "good daughter," the only child who cared.

Lois felt guilty when her mother was alone and in pain. Despite Lois' love for her mother and the feelings of guilt her mother triggered, Lois began feeling angry when she saw her mother becoming progressively more helpless and unwilling to take care of herself. Lois began to recognize that she was being taken advantage of by her mother's increasing dependency. But when Lois expressed her anger, her mother just became more tearful and helpless, and Lois felt more guilty, and the cycle repeated again. Only when Lois untangled herself from this interlocked system was her mother forced to achieve a healthier self-sufficiency.

SPECIAL PARENTING PROBLEMS

Most borderlines describe childhoods with characteristic features. Often, one parent was missing or frequently absent, had major commitments to outside affairs, hobby or career interests, or abused alcohol or drugs.

If both parents did live in the home, their relationship was usually not harmonious. There was often a lack of consensus about child rearing and, subsequently, one parent, usually the mother, assumed the primary parenting role. Such parents are rarely capable of presenting a united, collaborative front to their children. For such children, the world abounds with inconsistencies. When the child requires structure, he receives contradictions; when he needs firmness, he gets ambivalence. Thus, the future borderline is deprived of the opportunity to develop a consistent, core identity.

The mother of a borderline may be blatantly ill, but more often her pathology is quite subtle. She may even be perceived by others as the "perfect mother" because of her total "dedication" to her children. Further observation, however, reveals her overinvolvement in her children's lives, her encouragement of mutual dependencies, and her unwillingness to allow her children to mature and separate naturally.

Separations

Separations from parents, particularly during the first few years of life, are common in the borderline biography. On the surface, these separations may appear insignificant, yet they have profound effects. For example, the birth of a sibling takes the mother away from her normal activities for a few weeks, but when she returns, she is no longer as responsive to the older child—mother has disappeared and has been replaced by someone who will always be different, one who now has mothering duties with a younger sibling. For the healthy child in a healthy environment, this trauma is easily overcome, but for the borderline in a borderline setting it may be one of a series of losses and perceived abandonments. Extended illnesses, frequent travels, divorce, or the death of a parent also deprive the developing infant of consistent mothering at crucial times, which may interfere with his abilities to develop trust and constancy in his unstable and unreliable world.

The Trauma of Child Abuse

Severe physical and/or sexual abuse is a common trauma in the history of the borderline personality. When a child is abused, he invariably blames himself because (consciously or subconsciously) it is the best of the available alternatives. If he blames the adult, he will be terrified by his dependency on incompetents who are unable to take care of him. If he blames no one, pain becomes random and unpredictable and therefore even more frightening because he has no hope of controlling it. Blaming himself makes the abuse easier to understand and therefore possible to control—he can feel that he somehow causes the abuse and therefore will be able to find a way to end it; or he will give up and accept that he is "bad."

The borderline learns early in life that he is bad, that he causes bad things to happen. He begins to expect punishment and may only feel secure when being punished. Later, self-mutilation may sometimes be the borderline's way of perpetuating this familiar, secure feeling of being chastised. He may see abuse as a kind of love and repeat the abuse with his own children. As an adult he remains locked in the child's confusing world, in which love and hate co-mingle, only good and bad exist with no in between, and only inconsistency is consistent.

Abuse can take subtler forms than physical violence or deviant sexuality. Emotional abuse—expressed as verbal harassment, sarcasm, humiliation, or frigid silence—can be equally devastating. Stephanie, for example, could never please her father. When she was young, he called her "Chubby," and laughed at her clumsy tomboy attempts to please him by playing sports. She was "stupid" when her grades were less than perfect and when she broke dishes while trying to clear the kitchen. He ridiculed her strapless gown on prom night, and on graduation day, insisted that she would amount to nothing.

As an adult, Stephanie was always unsure of herself, never trusting flattering comments and hopelessly trying to please people who were impossible to please. After a long string of destructive relationships, Stephanie finally met Ted, who seemed caring and supportive. At every turn, however, Stephanie tried to sabotage the relationship, constantly testing his loyalty and questioning his commitment.

Ted needed to understand Stephanie's background and recognize that trust could not realistically be established except over long periods of time. Not everyone is willing to wait. Ted was.

Recognizing BPD in Adolescence

By definition, the struggles of adolescence and BPD are extremely similar: Both the normal adolescent and the borderline struggle for individuality and separation from parents, seek bonds with friends and identification with groups, try to avoid being alone, tend to go through dramatic mood changes, and are generally prone to impulsivity. The teenager's easy distractibility is analogous to the borderline's difficulty to commit himself to a goal and follow through. Adolescents' eccentric dress styles, prehistoric eating habits, and piercing music are usually attempts to carve out a distinctive identity and relate to specific groups of peers, efforts similar to those of borderlines.

A normal adolescent may listen to gloomy music, write pessimistic poetry, glorify suicidal celebrities, dramatically scream, cry, and threaten. However, the normal adolescent does not cut his wrists, binge and purge several times a day, become addicted to drugs, or attack his mother; and it is these extremes that herald BPD.

Some parents will deny the seriousness of an adolescent's problems (a drug overdose, for example) by dismissing them as a typical teenager's bid for attention. Though it is true that children often seek attention in dramatic ways, neither suicide attempts nor any destructive behaviors are "normal." They instead suggest the possibility of incipient borderline personality or another disorder and should be evaluated by a professional.

Usually others—parents, teachers, employers, friends—will recognize when the normal teenager crosses the border into borderline behavior, even before the adolescent himself. Continuous drug abuse, serial tumultuous relationships, or anorexic fasting are good indicators that deeper problems may be involved. The teen's whole style of functioning should be the focus of examination, rather than individual symptoms. This is especially crucial when considering the potential for suicide.

Suicide is the second leading cause of death among teenagers, after accidents, and is particularly prevalent in children who are depressed, abuse drugs, act impulsively, and have few support systems—all prominent features of BPD.[1] Threats of self-harm should always be taken seriously. Attempts to self-mutilate or harm oneself "only for attention" can go tragically awry. Parents who try to distinguish "real suicide" from "attention-seeking" miss the point—both are seriously pathological behaviors and require treatment, often hospitalization.

WORKING WITH THE BORDERLINE

In the work environment, borderlines are often perceived as "strange" or "eccentric": They may tend to isolate themselves, avoid personal contacts, and keep others away with an aura of surliness, suspicion, or eccentricity. Others habitually complain of physical ailments or personal problems, and occasionally have fits of paranoia and rage. Still others may act perfectly normal in the work situation, but appear awkward or uncomfortable around coworkers outside the workplace.

Over the last decade, many employers started Employee Assistant Programs (EAPs), in-house counselors and referral departments initially designed to help employees deal with alcohol and drug abuse problems. Today many EAPs are also available to help workers confront other emotional problems, as well as legal and financial difficulties. Although many EAP counselors are well-equipped to identify features of alcohol or drug abuse, or of prominent psychiatric illnesses such as depression or psychosis, they may be less familiar with the more intricate symptoms of BPD. Though the employee's supervisor, coworkers, counselor, even the employee himself may be aware of some dysfunctional or disruptive behaviors, the borderline might not be referred for treatment because his behaviors cannot be clearly associated with more familiar disorders.

The prospective employer may suspect borderline characteristics in an applicant who has a history of frequent job changes. These terminations will often be explained by "personality conflicts" (which, indeed, is often accurate). Other job separations may be sparked by a significant change—a new supervisor, new computer system, or an adjustment in job description—that disrupted a very structured (perhaps, even monotonous) routine.

Because the borderline may be very creative and dedicated, he may make a most valuable employee. When functioning on a higher level, he can be colorful, stimulating, and inspiring to others. Most borderlines, function optimally in a well-defined, structured environment in which expectations are clearly delineated.

Coworkers will be most comfortable with the borderline when they recognize his tendency to see the world as black or white and accept his need for well-defined structure. They should avoid "kidding around" with him and stay away from "good natured" mocking, which the borderline may often misconstrue. It may be helpful to intercede if the borderline becomes the target of others' jokes. Frequent compliments for good work, and matter-of-fact, noncondemning recognition of mistakes with suggestions for improvement can aid the borderline's functioning in the workplace.

Similarly, when the borderline is in an executive position, it is important for employees to recognize and learn to deal with his black-or-white thinking. Employees should learn to expect and accept his changeability with a minimum of hurt feelings. They should avoid entanglement in logical arguments, because consistency may not always be possible for the borderline. They should look for allies elsewhere in the organization to provide reliable feedback and evaluations.

PLAYING WITH THE BORDERLINE

At play the borderline is typically unpredictable and sometimes very disconcerting. He may have great difficulty with recreation and play with a seriousness that is out of proportion to the relaxed nature of the activity. He may be your newly assigned tennis doubles partner who at first seems nice enough, but as the game goes on becomes increasingly frustrated and angry. Though you continually remind him that "it's just a game," he may stomp around, curse himself, throw the racket, and swear to give up the sport. He may be your son's Little League coach who works well with the kids, but suddenly becomes wildly abusive to the teenage umpire or angrily humiliating to his own son—seen as an extension of himself—who strikes out with the bases loaded. Although these examples may describe borderline-like traits in some people who in fact are not borderline, when these behaviors are extreme or represent a consistent pattern, they may be indications of a true borderline personality.

The borderline's intensity interferes with his ability to relax and have fun. Others' attempts at humor may frustrate him and make him angry. It is virtually impossible "to kid him out of it." If you elect to continue playing tennis with your borderline partner, judicious use of SET principles may make the experience more tolerable.

THE MATURING BORDERLINE

Higher-functioning adult borderlines may have successful careers, assume traditional family roles, and have a cadre of friends and support systems. They may generally live satisfactory lives within their own separate corner of existence, despite recurrent frustrations with themselves and others who inhabit that niche.

Lower-functioning borderlines, however, have difficulty maintaining a job and friends and may lack family and support systems; they may inhabit lonelier and more desperate "black holes" within their own personal universe.

Common to all borderlines is an element of unpredictability and erratic behavior. It may be more obvious in the lonely isolate, but those who know the contented family man well can also detect inconsistencies in his behavior which belie the superficial rationality. At work even the borderline who is a successful businessman or professional may be known by those working closely with him to be a bit strange, if not mad, even if they can't quite localize what it is that projects that aura of imbalance.

As many borderlines grow older, they may "mellow out" to some degree. Impulsivity, mood swings, and self-destructive behaviors seem to diminish in dramatic intensity. This pattern might be an objective reflection of change or a subjective evaluation of those living and working with the borderline; the borderline's friends and lovers may have adjusted to his erratic actions over time and no longer notice or respond to the outrageousness.

Maybe it is because he has settled into a more routine lifestyle that no longer requires periodic outbursts—drinking binges, suicide threats, or other dramatic gestures—to achieve his needs. Perhaps with age the borderline loses the energy to maintain the frenetic pace of borderline living. Or perhaps there is simply a natural healing process that takes place for some borderlines as they mature. In any event, those sharing life with the borderline can expect his behaviors over time—maybe a very long time, and sometimes without treatment—to become more tolerable. At this point the unpredictable reactions become more predictable and therefore easier to manage, and it becomes possible for the borderline to learn how to love and be loved in a more healthy fashion.

Appendix A

DSM-III-R Axis Classifications

THIS APPENDIX LISTS diagnostic categories for psychiatric illnesses, as officially recognized by the *Diagnostic and Statistical Manual of Mental Disorders*, Third Edition-Revised (Washington, D.C.: American Psychiatric Association, 1987).

AXIS I DIAGNOSES

The following, a partial list of Axis I diagnoses, are primarily "state" disorders (see Chapter 2).

Disorders Usually First Evident in Infancy,
Childhood, or Adolescence:
   disruptive behavior disorders
      attention-deficit hyperactivity disorder
      conduct disorder
   anxiety disorders
   eating disorders
      anorexia nervosa
      bulimia nervosa
   tic disorders
      Tourette's

Organic Mental Disorders:
  dementias
    Alzheimer's

Psychoactive Substance Use Disorders:
  alcohol
  amphetamine
  cannabis
  cocaine
  hallucinogen
  opioid

Schizophrenia:
  catatonic
  disorganized
  paranoid
  undifferentiated

Psychotic Disorders Not Elsewhere Classified:
  brief reactive psychosis
  schizophreniform disorder
  schizoaffective disorder

Mood Disorders:
  bipolar disorder
  depressive disorder
    major depression
    dysthymia

Anxiety Disorders:
  panic disorder
  agoraphobia
  social phobia
  simple phobia
  obsessive compulsive disorder
  post-traumatic stress disorder
  generalized anxiety disorder

Somatoform Disorders:
  hypochondriasis
  conversion disorder

somatization disorder
somatoform pain disorder

Dissociative Disorders:
multiple personality disorder
psychogenic amnesia

Sexual Disorders:
exhibitionism
fetishism
voyeurism
pedophilia
erectile (impotence) disorder
inhibited orgasm
premature ejaculation
sexual masochism
sexual sadism

Sleep Disorders:
insomnia disorder
hypersomnia disorder

Factitious Disorders:
with physical symptoms
with psychological symptoms

Impulse Control Disorders:
intermittent explosive disorder
kleptomania
pathological gambling
pyromania

Adjustment Disorders:
with anxiety
with depression
with disturbance of conduct
with physical complaints

AXIS II DISORDERS (COMPLETE LISTING)

These Axis II disorders are personality ("trait") disorders.

Cluster A—People appear odd or eccentric.
  paranoid
  schizoid
  schizotypal

Cluster B—People appear dramatic, emotional, or erratic.
  antisocial
  borderline
  histrionic
  narcissistic

Cluster C—People appear anxious or fearful.

  avoidant
  dependent
  obsessive compulsive
  passive aggressive

Appendix B

Evolution of the
Borderline Syndrome

THE CONCEPT OF the borderline personality has evolved primarily through the theoretical formulations of psychoanalytic writers. Current DSM-III-R criteria—observable, objective, and statistically reliable principles for defining this disorder—are derived from the more abstract, speculative writings of psychoanalytic theorists over the past eighty years.

FREUD

During Freud's era at the turn of the century, psychiatry was a branch of medicine closely aligned with neurology. Psychiatric syndromes were defined by directly observable behaviors, as opposed to unobservable, mental, or "unconscious" mechanisms, and most forms of mental illness were attributed to neurophysiological aberrations.

Though Freud himself was an experienced neurophysiologist, he explored the mind through different portals. He developed the concept of the unconscious and initiated a legacy of psychological—rather than physiological—exploration of human behavior. Yet he remained convinced that physiological mechanisms would eventually be uncovered to coincide with his psychological theories.

Ninety years after Freud's landmark work, we have come

almost full circle: Today, diagnostic classifications are once again defined by observable phenomena, and new frontiers of research into borderline and other types of mental illness are again exploring neurophysiological factors (see Chapter 3), while not lessening the impact of psychological and environmental factors.

Freud's explication of the unconscious mind is the underpinning of psychoanalysis. He believed that psychopathology resulted from the conflict between primitive, unconscious impulses and the conscious mind's need to prevent these abhorrent, unacceptable thoughts from entering awareness. He first used hypnosis, and later "free association" and other classical psychoanalytical techniques, to explore his theories.

Ironically, Freud intended classical psychoanalysis to be primarily an investigative tool rather than a form of treatment. His colorful case histories—"The Rat Man," "The Wolf Man," "Little Hans," "Anna O," etc.—were published to support his evolving theories, not only to promote psychoanalysis as a treatment method. Many current psychiatrists believe that these patients, whom Freud felt exhibited hysteria and other types of neuroses, would today clearly be identified as borderline.

POST-FREUD PSYCHOANALYTIC WRITERS

Psychoanalysts who followed Freud were the main contributors to the modern concept of the borderline syndrome. In 1925, Wilhelm Reich's *The Impulsive Character* described attempts to apply psychoanalysis to certain unusual characterologic disorders that he encountered in his clinic. He found that the "impulsive character" was often immersed in two sharply contradictory feeling states at the same time but was able to maintain the states without apparent discomfort via the splitting mechanism—a concept that has become central to all subsequent theories on the borderline syndrome, particularly Kernberg's (see below).[1]

In the late twenties and early thirties, the followers of the British psychoanalyst Melanie Klein investigated the cases of many patients who seemed just beyond the reach of psychoanalysis. The Kleinians focused on psychological factors as opposed to biological-constitutional factors.

The term *borderline* was first coined by Adolph Stern in 1938 to describe a group of patients who did not seem to fit into the primary diagnostic classifications of "neuroses" and "psychoses."[2] These patients were obviously more ill than neurotic patients—in fact, "too ill for classical psychoanalysis,"—yet they did not, like psychotic patients, continually misinterpret the real world. Though, like neurotics, they displayed a wide range of anxiety symptoms, neurotic patients usually had a more solid, consistent sense of identity and used more mature coping mechanisms.

Throughout the forties and fifties, other psychoanalysts began to recognize a population of patients who did not fit existing pathological descriptions. Some patients appeared to be neurotic or mildly symptomatic, but when they engaged in traditional psychotherapy, especially psychoanalysis, they "unraveled." Similarly, hospitalization would also exacerbate symptoms and increase the patient's infantile behavior and dependency on the therapist and hospital.

Other patients would appear to be severely psychotic, often diagnosed schizophrenic, only to make a sudden and unexpected recovery within a very short time. (Such dramatic improvement is inconsistent with the usual course of schizophrenia.) Still other patients exhibited symptoms suggestive of depression, but their radical swings in mood did not fit the usual profile of depressive disorders.

Psychological testing also confirmed the presence of a new, unique classification. Certain patients performed normally on structured psychological tests (such as IQ tests), but on unstructured, projective tests requiring narrative personalized responses (such as the Rorschach [inkblot] test), their responses were much more akin to those of psychotic patients, who displayed thinking and fantasizing on a more regressed, more childlike level.

During this postwar period, psychoanalysts fastened onto different aspects of the syndrome, seeking to develop a succinct delineation. In many ways the situation was like the old tale of the blind men who stood around an elephant and touched its various anatomical parts, trying to identify it. Each man described a different animal, of course, depending on which part he touched. Similarly, researchers were able to touch and identify different aspects of the borderline syndrome but could not quite see the whole animal. Many researchers (Zilboorg, Hoch and Polatin, Bychowsky, and others)[3,4,5] and DSM-II (1968)[6] rallied around the schizophrenia-like aspects of the disorder, using such terms as "ambulatory schizophrenia," "pre-schizophrenic," "pseudoneurotic schizophrenia," and "latent schizophrenia" to describe these patients. Others concentrated on these patients' lack of a consistent, core sense of identity. In 1942, Helene Deutsch described a group of patients who overcame an intrinsic sense of emptiness by a chameleon-like altering of their internal and external emotional experiences to fit the people and situations they were involved with at the moment. She termed this tendency of adopting the qualities of others as a means of gaining or retaining their love the "as-if personality."[7]

In 1953, Robert Knight revitalized the term borderline in his consideration of "borderline states."[8] He recognized that, even though certain patients presented markedly different symptoms and were categorized with different diagnoses, they were expressing a common pathology.

After Knight's work was published, the term borderline became more popular, and the possibility of using Stern's general borderline concept as a diagnosis became more acceptable. In 1968, Roy Grinker and his colleagues defined four subtypes of the borderline patient: 1. a severely afflicted group who bordered on the psychotic; 2. a "core borderline" group with turbulent interpersonal relationships, intense feeling states, and loneliness; 3. an "as-if" group easily influenced by others and lacking in stable identity; and 4. a mildly impaired group with poor self-confidence and bordering on the neurotic end of the spectrum.[9]

Yet, even with all this extensive pioneering research, the diagnosis of borderline personality, among working clinicians, was still drenched in ambiguity. It was considered a "wastebasket diagnosis" by many, a place to "dump" those patients who were not well understood, who resisted therapy, or who simply did not get better; the situation remained that way well into the seventies.

As the borderline personality became more rigorously defined and distinguishable from other syndromes, attempts were made to change the ambiguous name. At one point, "unstable personality" was briefly considered during the development of DSM-III. However, borderline character pathology is relatively fixed and invariable despite its chaos—it is predictably stable in its instability. No other names have been prominently proposed as a replacement.

In the seventies, two major schools of thought evolved to delineate a consistent set of criteria for defining the borderline syndrome. Like some other disciplines in the natural and social sciences, psychiatry was split ideologically into two primary camps—one more concept-oriented; the other more influenced by descriptive, observable behavior that could be more easily retested and studied under laboratory conditions.

The empirical school, led by John Gunderson of Harvard and favored by many researchers, developed a structured, more behavioral definition, one that is based on observable criteria and thus more accessible to research and study. This definition is the most widely accepted and in 1980 was adopted by DSM-III (see Chapter 2).

The other more concept-oriented school, led by Otto Kernberg of Cornell and favored by many psychoanalysts, proposes a more psychostructural approach that describes the syndrome based on intrapsychic functioning and defense mechanisms rather than overt behaviors.

KERNBERG'S "BORDERLINE PERSONALITY ORGANIZATION" (BPO)

In 1967, Otto Kernberg introduced his concept of Borderline Personality Organization (BPO), a broader concept than DSM-III's Borderline Personality Disorder (BPD). Kernberg's conceptualization places BPO midway between neurotic and psychotic personality organization.[xii] A patient with BPO, as defined by Kernberg, is less impaired than a psychotic, whose perceptions of reality are severely contorted, making normal functioning impossible. On the other hand, the borderline is more disabled than a person with neurotic personality organization, who experiences intolerable anxiety as a result of emotional conflicts. The neurotic's perception of identity and system of defense mechanisms are usually more adaptive than those of the borderline.

BPO encompasses other Axis II, or characterological, disorders, such as paranoid, schizoid, antisocial, histrionic, and narcissistic personality disorders. In addition, it includes obsessive-compulsive and chronic anxiety disorders, hypochondriasis, phobias, sexual perversions, and dissociative reactions (such as multiple personality disorder).

In Kernberg's system, patients currently diagnosed with BPD would constitute only about 10 to 25 percent of patients classified BPO. A patient diagnosed with BPD is conceived as occupying a low-functioning, high-severity level within the overall BPO diagnosis.

Though Kernberg's system was not officially adopted by the APA, his work has had (and continues to have) enormous influence as a theoretical model for both clinicians and researchers. In general, Kernberg's schema emphasizes the inferred internal mechanisms discussed below:

Variable Sense of Reality

Like neurotics, borderlines retain contact with reality most of the time; however, under stress the borderline can regress to a brief psychotic state. (This trait is not recognized as an official criterion of BPD in DSM-III-R, but it is included in Gunderson's concept of BPD and was proposed, though not adopted, as a ninth criteria.)

Marjorie, a twenty-nine-year-old married woman, sought therapy for increasing depression and marital disharmony. An intelligent, attractive woman, Marjorie related calmly throughout her eight sessions. She eagerly assented to a joint interview with her husband, but during the session she turned uncharacteristically loud and belligerent. Dropping her facade of self-control, she began to berate her husband for alleged infidelities. She accused her therapist of taking her husband's side ("You men always stick together!") and accused both of engaging in a conspiracy against her. The sudden transformation from a relaxed, mildly depressed woman to a raging, paranoid one is quite characteristic of the kind of rapidly shifting borders of reality observed in the borderline.

Nonspecific Weaknesses in Functioning

Borderlines have great difficulty tolerating frustration and coping with anxiety. In Kernberg's framework, impulsive behavior is an attempt to diffuse this tension. Borderlines also have defective sublimation tools; that is, they are unable to channel frustrations and discomforts in socially adaptive ways. Though borderlines may display extreme empathy, warmth, and guilt, these exhibitions are often rote, more manipulative gestures for display purposes only rather than true expressions of feeling.

Indeed, the borderline may act as if he has totally forgotten a dramatic effusion that occurred only moments before, much like a child who suddenly emerges from a temper tantrum all smiles and laughter.

Primitive Thinking

Borderlines are capable of performing well in a structured work or professional environment, but below the surface linger grave self-doubts, suspiciousness, and fears. The internal thought processes of borderlines may be surprisingly unsophisticated and primal, camouflaged by a stable facade of learned and rehearsed platitudes. Any circumstance that pierces the protective structure shielding the borderline may unleash a flood of chaotic passions concealed within. The example of Marjorie (above) illustrates this point.

Projective psychological tests also reveal the borderline's primitive thought processes. These tests—such as the Rorschach and Thematic Apperception Test (TAT)—elicit associations to ambiguous stimuli, such as inkblots or pictures, around which the patient creates a story. Borderline responses typically resemble those of schizophrenics and other psychotic patients. Unlike the coherent, organized responses usually observed among neurotic patients, those from borderlines often describe bizarre, primitive images—the borderline might see vicious animals cannibalizing one another, where the neurotic sees a butterfly.

Primitive Defense Mechanisms

The coping mechanism of splitting (see Chapters 2 and 3) preserves the borderline's perception of a world of extremes—a view in which people and objects are either good or bad, friendly or hostile, loved or hated—in order to escape anxiety.

In Kernberg's conceptualization, splitting often leads to "magical thinking": Superstitions, phobias, obsessions, and compulsions are used as talismans to ward off unconscious fears. Splitting also results in derivative defense mechanisms:

- Primitive idealization—insistently placing a person or object in the "all good" category so as to avoid the anxiety

accompanying the recognition of faults in that person.
- Devaluation—an unrelenting negative view of a person or object; the opposite of idealization. Using this mechanism, the borderline avoids the guilt of his rage—the "all-bad" person fully deserves it.
- Omnipotence—a feeling of unlimited power in which one feels incapable of failure or sometimes even of death. (Omnipotence is also a common feature in the narcissistic personality.)
- Projection—disavowing features unacceptable to the self and attributing them to others.
- Projective identification—a more complex form of projection in which the projector continues an ongoing manipulative involvement with another person, who is the object of the projection. The other person "wears" these unacceptable characteristics for the projector, who works to insure their continued expression.

For example, Mark, a young, married man who is diagnosed as borderline finds his own sadistic and angry impulses unacceptable and projects them onto his wife, Sally. Sally is then perceived by Mark (in his black-and-white fashion) to be a "totally angry woman." All of her actions are interpreted as sadistic. He unconsciously "pushes her buttons" to extract angry responses, thus confirming his projections. In this way Sally is feared yet simultaneously controlled by Mark.

Pathological Concept of Self

"Identity diffusion" describes Kernberg's conception of the borderline's lack of a stable, core sense of identity. The borderline's identity is the consistency of jello: It can be molded into any configuration that contains it but slips through the hands when you try to pick it up. This lack of substance leads directly to the identity disturbances outlined in criterion 6 of DSM-III's description of BPD (see Chapter 2).

Pathological Concept of Others

As "identity diffusion" describes the borderline's lack of a stable concept of self, "object inconstancy" describes the lack of a stable concept of others. Just as his own self-esteem depends on current circumstances, the borderline bases his attitude toward another person on the most recent encounter rather than on a more stable and enduring perception grounded in a consistent, connected series of experiences.

Often, the borderline is unable to hold onto the memory of a person or object when he, she, or it is not present. Like a child who becomes attached to a transitional object that represents a soothing mother figure (such as Linus to his blanket), the borderline uses objects, such as pictures and clothing, to simulate the presence of another person. When a borderline is separated from home, for example, for even a brief period, he typically takes many personal objects as soothing reminders of home. Teddy bears and other stuffed animals accompany him to bed and snapshots of family are carefully placed around the room. If he is left home while his wife is away, he often stares longingly at her picture and her closet, smells her pillow, and so on.

For many borderlines, "out of sight, out of mind" is an excruciatingly real truism. Panic sets in when the borderline is separated from a loved one because the separation feels permanent. Because memory cannot be adequately utilized to retain an image, the borderline forgets what the object of his concern looks like, sounds like, feels like. To escape the panicky sensation of abandonment and loneliness, the borderline tries to cling desperately—calling, writing, using any means to maintain contact.

Appendix C

Medications Used to Treat BPD

MAJOR TRANQUILIZERS
(NEUROLEPTICS, ANTIPSYCHOTICS)

THIS CLASS OF medicines is used primarily to alleviate psychosis and to control destructive or paranoid behaviors and feelings of unreality. But these drugs may also help the nonpsychotic patient by quelling impulsive behaviors, angry and hostile outbursts, and severe agitation—all of which could be destructive to the patient or others. They also relieve throbbing anxiety states and sometimes reduce pain symptoms. The most common drugs in this class are: Thorazine (chlorpromazine), Stelazine (trifluoperazine), Trilafon (perphenazine), Mellaril (thioridazine), Serentil (mesoridazine), Haldol (haloperidol), Navane (thiothixene), Prolixin (fluphenazine), Loxitane (loxapine), Moban and Lidone (molindone).

Several recent studies have compared these drugs with placebos and antidepressants in treating borderline patients. In all of these studies neuroleptics provided greater improvement in all measured symptoms, including depression.[1]

Antidepressants

Depressive disorder is probably the most common diagnosis associated with BPD. When depression includes distinctive physical symptoms—such as changes in sleeping, eating, concentration, and energy—and when there is a strong family history of depression, antidepressant medicines often improve symptoms dramatically. Complicating the picture, however, are reports that some borderlines actually get worse with antidepressants.[2]

There are several classes of antidepressants:

Cyclic antidepressants. These are some of the oldest and most commonly employed antidepressants. (Cyclic refers to the rings in the molecular structure of the drug prototype.) These include Elavil (amitriptylene), Pamelor and Aventyl (nortriptylene), Vivactil (protriptylene), Tofranil (imipramine), Sinequan and Adapin (doxepin), Norpramin and Pertofrane (desipramine), Desyrel (trazodone), Ludiomil (maprotilene), Asendin (amoxapine), Surmontil (trimipramine), and Prozac (fluoxetine).

Monoamine oxidase (MAO) inhibitors. This group of antidepressants is utilized less frequently partly because these drugs may precipitate dangerous episodes of high blood pressure when mixed with certain medications (such as decongestants, diet pills, or some analgesics, such as demerol) or with certain foods (such as aged cheeses, some wines and other alcoholic drinks, chicken livers, etc.). Patients on MAO inhibitors, therefore, must reliably follow a certain diet. The most common MAO inhibitors are Nardil (phenelzine) and Parnate (tranylcypromine).

MAO inhibitors seem to be more beneficial for patients with atypical features of depression, such as difficulty falling asleep, increased appetite, marked sensitivity to rejection, and mood changes associated with changes in situation. In contrast, typical depression is more usually characterized by middle-of-the-night insomnia (after easily falling asleep initially), decreased appetite, and less vulnerability to situational changes. Many borderlines experience atypical signs.

Both cyclic antidepressants and MAO inhibitors are sometimes used to treat other symptoms, such as primary anxiety, phobias, obsessive-compulsive disorders, and some pain syndromes.

Lithium. Lithium, most commonly associated with manic-depressive illness, provides benefit for borderline patients who exhibit depression or precipitous swings in mood. Lithium has also been proven useful in treating impulsive and aggressive behaviors. Some studies have suggested that lithium is an effective medication for alcoholism.

Psychostimulants. This class of drugs, used less frequently in treating depression, includes Ritalin (methylphenidate), Dexedrine (dextroamphetamine), and Cylert (pemoline). These medicines have also proven effective in treating attention-deficit disorder (hyperactivity), which is usually diagnosed in children but sometimes persists into adulthood. In this syndrome patients are often physically clumsy and have difficulty concentrating, sitting still, and attending to one task and seeing it through to completion.

Electroconvulsive treatment (ECT). Despite continued controversy regarding its use, ECT remains one of the most effective therapies for depression, with a higher response rate than even antidepressant medicines. It remains a relatively safe procedure, despite the necessity for accompanying anesthesia. In contrast to some anecdotal claims, none of the many scientific studies have ever demonstrated any anatomical evidence of brain damage resulting from ECT. There is, however, frequent temporary or permanent short-term memory loss that occurs at the time of ECT administration. This usually clears over time, but the acute memory dysfunction interferes with psychotherapy and is the major drawback to using ECT in treating depression in a patient who also requires concomitant psychotherapy.

Anti-Anxiety Agents

Minor Tranquilizers. This group of drugs is designed to treat the omnipresent anxiety that often relentlessly pursues the borderline. The earliest progenitors in this group were the barbiturates (Seconal, Nembutal, Pentothal, Amytal). Later entries included Equanil and Miltown (meprobamate), Placidyl (ethchlorvynol), Doriden (glutethimide), Quaalude and Sopor (methaqualone), Noludar (methyprylon), Noctec (chloral hydrate). All of these drugs are highly addictive, can precipitate dangerous with-drawal when stopped, are lethal in higher doses, and are not optimally effective in treating anxiety. Benadryl (di-phenhydramine), Paral (paraldehyde), Phenergan (pro-methazine), Vistaril and Atarax (hydroxyzine) are somewhat less toxic, but also less effective.

Benzodiazepines. This group of drugs, first synthesized thirty years ago, has proved to be more valuable in relieving anxiety symptoms. Although these medicines may induce dependency and subsequent withdrawal phenomena, they are less toxic with overdosage. Librium (chlordiazepoxide), Valium (diazepam), Xanax (alprazolam), Tranxene (chlorazepate), Serax (oxaze-pam), Klonopin (clonazepam), Paxipam (halazepam), Centrax (prazepam) are in this category.

Although many studies have cited the usefulness of ben-zodiazepines in treating BPD, a few have noted that some bor-derline patients react to these drugs with greater impulsivity, aggression, and loss of control.[34]

Buspar (buspirone) is a recently developed drug for anxiety that appears to have fewer side effects, including less sedation and less propensity for addiction. Its efficacy with borderlines is not as clearly established.

Beta-Blockers. Some of the body's automatic responses to anxiety—palpitations, rapid heartbeat, tremors, sweating, and muscle twitching—are caused by the secretion of hormones, such as adrenalin. Medicines called beta-blockers interfere with the release of these substances and relieve some of these com-ponents of anxiety. Inderal (propranolol) is the most commonly used beta-blocker. This group of drugs is used less frequently for BPD.

Anticonvulsants

Because the borderline's impulsivity, mood swings, rageful out-bursts, and uncontrollable behavior sometimes resemble epilepsy or other neurological disorders, some psychiatrists rec-ommend anti-seizure medicine for treating BPD. In addition, some studies have documented abnormal EEGs (brain-wave tests) in a significant group of borderline patients.[56] Tegretol (carbamazepine) is the anticonvulsant that has been most extensively investigated, thus far. Some studies indicate that this drug improves the borderline's ability to control impulsive outbursts.[7] [8] Other anticonvulsants, such as dilantin (diphenylhydantoin) and depakene (valproate) have been suggested but not yet adequately studied.

For Further Exploration

The following organizations provide materials, services, or information for consumers on BPD and mental health in general.

National Alliance for the Mentally Ill
1901 North Fort Myer Drive
Suite 500
Arlington, Virginia 22209

National Mental Health Consumers' Association
311 South Juniper Street
Room 902
Philadelphia,PA 19107

Notes

CHAPTER 1: THE WORLD OF THE BORDERLINE

1. A. Loranger, J. Oldham, and E. Tulis, "Familial Transmission of DSM-III Borderline Personality Disorder," *Archives of General Psychiatry* 39 (1982): 795-799.

2. Miron Baron et al., "Familial Transmission of Schizotypal and Borderline Personality Disorders," *American Journal of Psychiatry* 142 (1985): 927-934.

3. John G. Gunderson, *Borderline Personality Disorder* (Washington, D.C.: American Psychiatric Press, 1984).

4. Minna R. Fyer et al., "Comorbidity of Borderline Personality Disorder," *Archives of General Psychiatry* 45 (1988): 348-352.

5. Craig Johnson, David Tobin, and Amy Enright, "Prevalence and Clinical Characteristics of Borderline Patients in an Eating-Disordered Population," *Journal of Clincal Psychiatry* 50 (1989): 9-15

6. Edgar P. Nace, J. Saxon, and N. Shore, "A Comparison of Borderline and Non-Borderline Alcoholic Patients," *Archives of General Psychiatry* 40 (1983): 54-56.

7. David J. Inman, Loy O. Bascue, and Thomas Skoloda, "Identification of Borderline Personality Disorders Among Substance Abuse Inpatients," *Journal of Substance Abuse Treatment* 2 (1985): 229-232.

8. Michael H. Stone, David K. Stone, and Stephen W. Hurt, "Natural History of Borderline Patients Treated by Intensive Hospitalization," *Psychiatric Clinics of North America* 10 (1987): 185-206.

9. American Psychiatric Association: *Diagnostic and Statistical Manual of Mental Disorders*, 3rd-revised ed. (Washington, D.C.: American Psychiatric Association, 1987), 346-347.

10. Craig Johnson, David Tobin and Amy Enright, "Prevelance and Clinical Characteristics of Borderline Patients in an Eating-Disordered Population," *Journal of Clinical Psychiatry* 50 (1989) pp. 9-15.

11. Jeffrey B. Bryer et al., "Childhood Sexual and Physical Abuse as Factors in Adult Psychiatric Illness," *American Journal of Psychiatry* 144 (1987): 426-430.

12. Hagop S. Akiskal, "Subaffective Disorders: Dysthymic, Cyclothymic, and Bipolar II Disorders in the Borderline Realm," *Psychiatric Clinics of North America* 4 (1981): 25-46.

13. Margaret Mahler, F. Pine, and A. Bergman, *The Psychological Birth of the Human Infant* (New York: Basic Books, 1975).

14. Katherine A. Henry and Carl I. Cohen, "The Role of Labeling Processes in Diagnosing Borderline Personality Disorder," *American Journal of Psychiatry* 140 (1983): 1527-1529.

15. Ricardo Castaneda and Hugo Franco, "Sex and Ethnic Distribution of Borderline Personality Disorders in an Inpatient Sample," *American Journal of Psychiatry* 142 (1985): 1202-1203.

16. Thomas H. McGlashan, "The Chestnut Lodge Follow-Up Study III, Long-term Outcome of Borderline Personalities," *Archives of General Psychiatry* 43 (1986): 20-30.

17. Joel Sadavoy and Barbara Dorian, "Treatment of the Elderly Characterologically Disturbed Patient in the Chronic Care Institution," *Journal of Geriatric Psychiatry* 16 (1983): 223-240.

18. Daniel J. Siegel and Gary W. Small, "Borderline Personality Disorder in the Elderly: A Case Study," *Canadian Journal of Psychiatry* 31 (1986): 859-860.

19. Louis Sass, "The Borderline Personality," *New York Times Magazine*, Aug. 22, 1982.

CHAPTER 2: CHAOS AND EMPTINESS

1. Owen D. Buck, "Multiple Personality as a Borderline State," *The Journal of Nervous and Mental Disease* 171 (1983): 62-65.

2. David G. Benner and Brenda Joscelyne, "Multiple Personality as a Borderline Disorder," *The Journal of Nervous and Mental Disease* 172 (1984): 98-104.

3. William F. Clary, Kenneth J. Burstin, and John S. Carpenter, "Multiple Personality and Borderline Personality Disorder," *Psychiatric Clinics of North America* 7 (1984): 89-99.

4. E. L. Bliss, "Multiple Personality: A Report of 14 Cases with Implications for Schizophrenia and Hysteria," *Archives of General Psychiatry* 36 (1980): 1388-1397.

5. Richard P. Horevitz and Bennett G. Braun, "Are Multiple Personalities Borderline?" *Psychiatric Clinics of North America* 7 (1984) 69-87.

6. Vicki Westherford, paper presented at the Annual Meeting of the American Psychiatric Association, May, 1988.

7. Edgar P. Nace (1983), 54-56.

8. David J. Inman (1985): 229-232.

9. Hilda Bruch, "Four Decades of Eating Disorders," in *Handbook of Psychotherapy for Anorexia and Bulimia*, eds. David M. Garner and Paul E. Garfinkle (New York: Guilford Press, 1985), 7-18.

10. Craig Johnson, David Towbin and Amy Enright, "Prevelance and Clinical Characteristics of Borderline Patients in an Eating-Disordered Population," *Journal of Clinical Psychiatry* 50 (1989) pp. 9-15.

11. Regina C. Casper et al., "Bulimia: Its Incidence and Clinical Importance in Patients with Anorexia Nervosa," *Archives of General Psychiatry* 37 (1980): 1030-1035.

12. Centers for Disease Control, *Suicide Surveillance, 1970-1980* (Atlanta: U.S. Dept. of Health and Human Services, 1985).

13. D. Shaffer and P. Fisher, "The Epidemiology of Suicide in Children and Young Adolescents," *Journal of the American Academy of Child Psychiatry* 20 (1981): 545-565.

14. Gerald L. Klerman, "Clinical Epidemiology of Suicide," *Journal of Clinical Psychiatry* 48 supp. (1987): 33-53.

15. American Psychiatric Association, DSM-III-R (1987), 346-347.

16. John G. Gunderson and Margaret T. Singer, "Defining Borderline Patients: An Overview," *American Journal of Psychiatry* 132 (1975): 1-10.

17. John G. Gunderson and Jonathan E. Kolb, "Discriminating Features of Borderline Patients," *American Journal of Psychiatry* 135 (1978): 792-796.

18. Octavio Paz, *The Endless Instant* (1966).

19. E. Nowell, *Thomas Wolfe, A Biography* (New York: Doubleday, 1960), 167.

20. Norman Mailer, *Marilyn* (New York: Grosset & Dunlap, 1973), 86.

21. Ibid, 108.

22. George S. Zubenko et al., "Sexual Practices Among Patients with Borderline Personality Disorder," *American Journal of Psychiatry* 144 (1987): 748-752.

23. Graham Greene, *A Sort of Life* (New York: Simon and Schuster, 1971).

24. Norman Rosten, *Marilyn: An Untold Story* (New York: New American Library, 1967), 112.

25. Gloria Steinem, *Marilyn* (New York: New American Library, 1986), 154.

CHAPTER 3: ROOTS OF THE BORDERLINE SYNDROME

1. James F. Masterson, *The Narcissistic and Borderline Disorders: an Integrated Developmental Approach* (New York: Brunner/Mazell, 1981), 131-133.

2. Margaret S. Mahler (1975).

3. A Letter from T. E. Lawrence to Charlotte Shaw, August 18, 1927, as quoted by John E. Mack, A Prince of Our Disorder: The Life of T. E. Lawrence (Boston: Little, Brown and Co., 1976), 31.

4. Norman Mailer (1973).

5. Ibid, 36.

6. Norman Rosten (1967), 89.

7. John G. Gunderson, John Kerr, and Diane Woods Englund, "The Families of Borderlines: A Comparative Study," *Archives of General Psychiatry* 37 (1980): 27-33.

8. Hallie Frank and Joel Paris, "Recollections of Family Experience In Borderline Patients," *Archives of General Psychiatry* 38 (1981): 1031-1034.

9. Ronald B. Feldman and Herta A. Guttman, "Families of Borderline Patients: Literal Minded Parents, Borderline Parents, and Parental Protectiveness," *American Journal of Psychiatry* 141 (1984): 1392-1396.

10. Stewart A. Montgomery, "The Psychopharmacology of Borderline Disorders," *ACTA of Psychiatry of Belgium* 87 supp. (1987): 260-266.

11. Paul H. Soloff, *Journal of Clinical Psychiatry* 48 supp. (1987): 13.

12. Paul A. Andrulonis et al., "Organic Brain Dysfunction and the Borderline Syndrome," *Psychiatric Clinics of North America* 4 (1980): 47-66.

13. Scott Snyder and W. N. Pitts, Jr., "Electroencephalography of DSM III Borderline Personality Disorder," *ACTA of Psychiatry of Scandinavia* 69 (1984): 129 ff.

14. J. Bell et al., "Effect of Pre-Existing Borderline Personality Disorder on Clinical and EEG Sleep Correlates of Depression," *Psychiatry Resources* 9 (1983):

15. C. F. Reynolds III et al., "Depression in Borderline Cases: A Prospective EEG Study," *Psychiatry Resources* 14 (1985): 1-15.

16. Hagop Akiskal et al., "The Nosologic Status of Borderline Personality: Clinical and Polysomnographic Study," *American Journal of Psychiatry* 142 (1985): 192-198.

17. Harrison G. Pope, Jr. et al., "The Validity of DSM III Borderline Personality Disorder: A Phenomenologic, Family History, Treatment Response and Long Term Follow-Up Study," *Archives of General Psychiatry* 40 (1983): 23-30.

18. Paul H. Soloff and James Millward, "Psychiatric Disorders in the Families of Borderline Patients," *Archives of General Psychiatry* 40 (1983): 37-44.

19. Miron Baron (1985): 927-934.

20. Seymour S. Kety et al., "The Types and Problems of Mental Illness in the Biological and Adoptive Families of Adopted Schizophrenics," in *The Transmission of Schizophrenia*, eds. David Rosenthal and Seymour S. Kety (Oxford: Pergamon Press, 1968): 345-362.

21. Michael H. Stone, "The Borderline Syndrome: Evolution of the Term, Genetic Aspects and Prognosis," *American Journal of Psychotherapy* 31 (1977): 345-365.

22. Thomas A. Aronson, "Historical Perspectives on the Borderline Concept: A Review and Critique," *Psychiatry* 48 (1985): 209-222.

CHAPTER 4: THE BORDERLINE SOCIETY

1. Christopher Lasch, *The Culture of Narcissism* (New York: W. W. Norton, 1978), 34.

2. Louis Sass (1982), 13.

3. Peter L. Giovachinni, *Psychoanalysis of Character Disorders* (New York: Jason Aronson, 1975).

4. Christopher Lasch (1978), 5.

5. David S. Greenwald, *No Reason to Talk About It* (New York: Norton, 1987).

6. Paul A. Andrulonis, personal communication, 1987.

7. Nancy Traub, "Supertots: The Collapse of Childhood," *Diablo*, June, 1987.

8. T. Berry Brazelton, "Issues of Working Parents," *American Journal of Orthopsychiatry* 56 (1986):15.

9. Christopher Lasch (1978), 30.

10. Ricardo Castaneda (1985), 1202-1203.

11. George S. Zubenko (1987), 748-752.

12. Otto Kernberg, "Borderline Personality Organization," *Journal of the American Psychoanalytic Association* 15 (1967): 642-685.

13. Brazelton (1986), 15.

14. Thomas J. Gamble & Edward Zigler, "Effects of Infant Day Care: Another Look at the Evidence," *American Journal of Orthopsychiatry* 56 (1986): 26-42.

15. Edward F. Zigler, "A Solution to the Nation's Child Care Crisis," paper presented at the National Health Policy Forum, Washington, D.C. (1987), 1.

16. Cecilia M. Lilliston, "Child Sexual Abuse: An Advocacy-Outreach Treat ment Model," American Orthopsychiatric Association paper, Annual Conference, 1987.

17. James F. Masterson, *The Real Self: A Developmental, Self, and Object Relations Approach* (New York: Brunner/Mazel, 1985).

18. Brazelton (1986), 26-42.

19. Brazelton (1986), 20.

20. Brazelton (1986), 14.

21. Brazelton (1986), 22-23.

22. Betty Holcomb, "Where's Mommy? The Great Debate over the Effects of Day Care," *New York*, April 13, 1987, p. 75.

23. Hal Straus, "The Day Care Dilemma" *American Health*, Sept. 1988, p.61.

24. Vincent J. Fontana, "Child Maltreatment and Battered Child Syndromes," in *Comprehensive Textbook of Psychiatry*, 4th ed., ed. Harold I. Kaplan and Benjamin J. Sadock (Baltimore: Williams & Wilkins, 1985), 1816.

25. Judith L. Herman, *Father-Daughter Incest* (Cambridge, Mass.: Harvard University Press, 1981).

26. Lawrence Claman and J.J. Stephens, "Improving Intervention Services for Preschool-Age Child Victims of Physical Abuse and Neglect," paper presented at American Orthopsychiatric Association meeting, 1988.

27. Susan Jacoby, "Emotional Child Abuse: The Invisible Plague," Glamour , October 1984; Edna J. Hunter, quoted in *USA Today*, August 1985, 11.

28. W. Hugh Missildine, *Your Inner Child of the Past* (New York: Simon and Shuster, 1963).

29. Judith Wallerstein and J. B. Kelly, "The Effect of Parental Divorce: Experiences of the Preschool Child," *Journal of the American Academy of Child Psychiatry* 14 (1975):600-616.

30. Ibid.

31. M. Hetherington, "Children and Divorce," in *Parent-Child Interaction: Theory, Research, and Prospect*, ed. R. Henderson (New York: Academic Press, 1981).

32. Chaim F. Shatan, "Through the Membrane of Reality: 'Impacted Grief' and Perceptual Dissonance in Vietnam Combat Veterans," *Psychiatric Opinion* 11 (1982): 6-15.

33. Chaim F. Shatan, "The Tattered Ego of Survivors," *Psychiatric Annals* 12 (1982): 1031-1038.

34. Chaim F. Shatan, "War Babies," *American Journal of Orthopsychiatry* 45 (1975): 289.

35. Paul Andrulonis (1987).

CHAPTER 7: SEEKING THERAPY

1. John G. Gunderson, *Borderline Personality Disorder* (Washington D.C.: American Psychiatric Press, 1984), 77.

2. Otto Kernberg, *Borderline Conditions and Pathological Narcissism* (New York: Jason Aronson, 1975).

3. James F. Masterson, *Psychotherapy of the Borderline Adult* (New York: Brunner/Mazel, 1976).

4. William Goldstein, *An Introduction to the Borderline Conditions* (New York: Jason Aronson, 1985), 201-203. Also, Gunderson (1984), 51-52.

5. Norman Rosten (1972), 100.

6. Ibid, 100-101.

7. Norman D. Macaskill, "Therapeutic Factors in Group Therapy with Borderline Patients," *International Journal of Group Psychotherapy* 32 (1) (1982): 61-73.

8. Wendy Froberg and Brent D. Slife, "Overcoming Obstacles to the Implementation of Yalom's Model of Inpatient Group Psychotherapy," *International Journal of Group Psychotherapy* 37 (3) (1987): 371-388.

9. Leonard Horwitz, "Indications for Group Therapy with Borderline and Narcissistic Patients," *Bulletin of the Menninger Clinic* 1 (3) (1987): 248-260.

10. Gunderson (1984), 170-172.

11. Stephen A. Jones, "Family Therapy with Borderline and Narcissistic Patients," *Bulletin of the Menninger Clinic* 51 (3) (1987): 285-295.

12. Gunderson (1984), 162-169.

13. Paul H. Soloff, "A Pharmacologic Approach to the Borderline Patient," *Psychiatric Annals* 17 (3) (1987): 201-205.

14. Phillip A. Berger, "Pharmacological Treatment for Borderline Personality Disorder," *Bulletin of the Menninger Clinic* 51 (3) (1987): 277-284.

15. Rex W. Cowdry and David L. Gardner, "Pharmacotherapy of Borderline Personality Disorder," *Archives of General Psychiatry* 45 (1988): 111-119.

16. Gunderson (1984).

17. Michael Rosenbluth, "The Inpatient Treatment of the Borderline Personality Disorder: A Critical Review and Discussion of Aftercare Implications," *Canadian Journal of Psychiatry* 32 (1987): 228-237.

18. Daniel H. Jacobs et al., "The Neglected Alliance: The Inpatient Unit as a Consultant to Referring Therapists," *Hospital and Community Psychiatry* 33 (5) (1982): 377-381.

19. Jerold J. Kreisman, "CTU: The Systematic Inpatient Treatment of the Borderline Patient," *Res Medica* 3 (2) (1986): 19-26.

20. Daniel Silver, Robert J. Cardish, and Edward J. Glassman, "Intensive Treatment of Characterologically Difficult Patients: A General Hospital Perspective," *Psychiatric Clinics of North America* 10 (2) (1987): 219-245.

21. Maetin Pildis et al., "Day Hospital Treatment of Borderline Patients: A Clinical Perspective," *American Journal of Psychiatry* 135 (5) (1978): 594-596.

22. Alan B. Eppel and Mary Thomas Dart, "Day Hospital Treatment of the Borderline," paper presented at the Annual Meeting of the American Psychiatric Association, May 1985.

23. Han Soo Lee, "Patients' Comments on Psychiatric Inpatient Treatment Exxperiences: Patient-Therapist Relationships and Their Implications for Treatment Outcome," *Psychiatric Quarterly* 51 (1) (1979): 39-54.

24. Robert J. Waldinger and John G. Gunderson, "Completed Psychotherapies with Borderline Patients," *American Journal of Psychotherapy* 38 (1984): 190-202.

25. Michael H. Stone, David K. Stone, and Stephen W. Hurt, "Natural History of Borderline Patients Treated by Intensive Hospitalization," *Psychiatric Clinics of North America* 10 (2) (1987): 185-206.

26. Robert J. Waldinger and John G. Gunderson, *Effective Psychotherapy with Borderline Patients: Case Studies* (New York: Macmillan Publishing Company, 1987).

CHAPTER 8: COPING WITH THE BORDERLINE

1. David A. Brent et al., "Risk Factors for Adolescent Suicide," *Archives of General Psychiatry* 45 (June, 1988): 581-588.

APPENDIX B: EVOLUTION OF THE BORDERLINE SYNDROME

1. Michael H. Stone, "The Borderline Syndrome: Evolution of the Term, Genetic Aspects and Prognosis," *American Journal of Psychotherapy* 31 (1977): 345-365.

2. Adolph Stern, "Psychoanalytic Investigation of and Therapy in the Border Line Group of Neuroses," *The Psychoanalytic Quarterly* 7 (1938): 467-489.

3. G. Zilboorg, "Ambulatory Schizophrenia," *Psychiatry* 4 (1941): 149-155.

4. Paul Hoch and Philip Polatin, "Pseudoneurotic Forms of Schizophrenia," *Psychiatric Quarterly* 23 (1949): 248-276.

5. G. Bychowski, "The Problem of Latent Psychosis," *Journal of the American Psychoanalytic Association* 4 (1953): 484-503.

6. *Diagnostic & Statistical Manual of Mental Disorders*, 2nd edition (Washington, D.C.: American Psychiatric Association, 1968).

7. Helene Deutsch, "Some Forms of Emotional Disturbance and the Relationship to Schizophrenia," *The Psychoanalytic Quarterly* 11 (1942): 301-321.

8. Robert P. Knight, "Borderline States," *Bulletin of the Menninger Clinic* 17 (1953): 1-12.

9. Roy R. Grinker, B. Werble, and R. C. Drye, *The Borderline Syndrome* (New York: Basic Books, 1968).

10. Otto Kernberg, "Borderline Personality Organization," *Journal of the Psychoanalytic Association* 15 (1967): 641-685.

11. Otto Kernberg, *Borderline Conditions and Pathological Narcissism* (New York: Jason Aronson, 1975).
Psychiatric Quarterly 23 (1949): 248-276.

5. G. Bychowski, "The Problem of Latent Psychosis," Journal of the American Psychoanalytic Association 4 (1953): 484-503.

6. American Psychiatric Association, DSM-III-R .

7. Helene Deutsch, "Some Forms of Emotional Disturbance and the Relationship to Schizophrenia," The Psychoanalytic Quarterly 11 (1942): 301-321.

8. Robert P. Knight, "Borderline States," Bulletin of the Menninger Clinic 17 (1953): 1-12.

9. Roy R. Grinker, B. Werble, and R. C. Drye, The Borderline Syndrome (New York: Basic Books, 1968).

10. Otto Kernberg, "Borderline Personality Organization," Journal of the Psychoanalytic Association 15 (1967): 641-685.

11. Otto Kernberg, Borderline Conditions and Pathological Narcissism (New York: Jason Aronson, 1975).

APPENDIX C: MEDICATIONS USED TO TREAT BPD

1. Paul H. Soloff, Anselm George, and R. Swami Nathan, "Progress in Pharmacotherapy in Borderline Disorders," *Archives of General Psychiatry* (43) (1986): 691-697.

2. Paul H. Soloff, Anselm George, and R. Swami Nathan, "Paradoxical Effects of Amitriptyline on Borderline Patients," *American Journal of Psychiatry* 143 (1986): 1603-1605.

3. Frank J. Faltus, "The Positive Effect of Alprazolam in the Treatment of Three Patients with Borderline Personality Disorder," *American Journal of Psychiatry* 141 (6) (1984): 802-803.

4. R. Gaind and R. Jacoby, "Benzodiazepines Causing Aggression," in Vol. 1 *Current Themes in Psychiatry*, eds. R. Gaind and B. L. Hudson (London: Macmillan Publishing Company, 1978), 371-379.

5. Scott Snyder and Wesley M. Pitts, Jr., "Electroencephalography of DSM-III Borderline Personality Disorder," *Acta Psychiatry, Scandinavia* 69 (1984): 129-134.

6. Jack R. Cornelius et al., "EEG Abnormalities in Borderline Personality Disorder: Specific or Non-Specific," *Biological Psychiatry* 21 (1986): 977-980.

7. David L. Gardner and Rex W. Cowdry, "Positive Effects of Carbamazepine on Behavioral Dyscontrol in Borderline Personality Disorder," *American Journal of Psychiatry* 143 (4) (1986): 519-522.

8. David L. Gardner and Rex W. Cowdry, "Anticonvulsants in Personality Disorders," in Use of Anticonvulsants in Psychiatry: Recent Advances , eds. Susan L. McElroy and Harrison G. Pope (Clifton, N.J.: Oxford Health Care, 1988), 127-140.

Index